Spring Cloud Fundamentals

Dedicated to my son Ayaan

Author information

For any help please contact :
Amazon Author Page :
amazon.com/author/ajaykumar
Email : ajaycucek@gmail.com ,
 ajaxreso@gmail.com
Linkedin :
https://www.linkedin.com/in/ajaycucek
Facebook :
https://www.facebook.com/ajaycucek
Youtube :
 https://www.youtube.com/channel/UC1uXEe
btqCLYxVdzirKZGIA
Twitter : https://twitter.com/ajaycucek
Instagram :
https://www.instagram.com/ajaycucek/
Skype : ajaycucek

Table of contents

Module 1: Course Overview

The cloud, or cloud computing, is truly changing the way we, as developers, think about design and develop software. And that's where Spring Cloud comes in. Spring Cloud helps you take full advantage of these new paradigms by bringing together the best of Spring Boot with proven cloud strategies to help you design and develop cloud-native applications. Some of the major topics we'll cover include service discovery using Spring Cloud and Netflix Eureka, distributed configuration using Spring Cloud Config Server, client-side load balancing using Spring Cloud and Netflix Ribbon, intelligent routing via a gateway service using Spring Cloud and Netflix Zuul, and fault tolerance using Spring Cloud and Netflix Hystrix. By the end of this book, you'll know how to build applications that take full advantage of the cloud. Before beginning the book, you should be familiar with Java, Spring Boot, and have at least an introductory level understanding of microservices.

Module 2: Getting Familiar with Spring Cloud

The Infamous Cloud

I'm sure you've heard of this infamous thing called the cloud as it's often hyped as this game changer or the sort of magical solution to everything. It'll solve all your problems. And with so many things to learn these days, it's hard not to ignore a lot of that and just kind of brush it off as clever marketing. But now companies and enterprises are finally starting to truly embrace the cloud, and some of that hype is actually becoming a reality. And it's more often the norm to see enterprises and companies using the cloud than it is the exception. As software engineers, I think we have some really exciting times ahead of us. Cloud computing, or the cloud, is really changing the way that we build software. We're moving from using these centralized monoliths to applications which are distributed and use microservices. And not only is the software changing, but the hardware is changing as well. We're moving from this managed and finite resource to this infinite and on demand and self-service resource.

New Challenges with the Cloud

With the cloud, there comes these new challenges. We have to think differently. Things are not quite as static as we're used to, and we can't just design and architect and use the same principles or techniques that we're used to. The cloud is this elastic and ephemeral thing. Things can grow and shrink and appear and disappear at any given time. So we have to consider that the cloud is this ever-changing and constantly evolving thing, whereas we may be used to something that is a bit more static. We also can't just move our existing applications to the cloud and expect them to be automatically cloud enabled. This is often referred to as the lift and shift migration. And sure we're going to get some benefits by moving to the cloud, but we're not fully utilizing the cloud. In order to fully utilize the cloud, it requires change. And that's where Spring Cloud helps. Spring Cloud helps you build cloud-native applications. Now, you're probably asking what is a cloud-native application? Well, a cloud-native application means that your application was specifically built and engineered for the cloud. It means your application fully utilizes all of the cloud computing paradigms. Spring Cloud itself is not actually a framework. Loosely speaking, Spring Cloud is used to describe a number of projects that all fall under the same umbrella. In this book, we'll focus on the fundamentals,

which is Spring Cloud Config and Spring
Cloud Netflix.

Your Focus for the book

- Service Discovery
- Distributed
- Configuration
- Intelligent Routing
- Client-side Load Balancing
- Circuit Breaker

We're going to specifically target a number of
key areas. First, we're going to look at service
discovery. How do you dynamically find your
application services in the cloud at runtime?
Then, we'll move on to distributed
configuration, or how to manage common or
service-specific configuration in a distributed
system. Then, we'll look at intelligent routing,
or how to make a distributed system look as if
it were a single cohesive system using
Intelligent Routing. Then, we'll look at client-
side load balancing, or how you distribute
load among several instances of the same
service. And last, we'll look at how you can use
the circuit breaker pattern to build fault-
tolerant applications in the cloud.

Prerequisites

- Java 8+
- Spring Boot 1.4+
- Knowledge of Microservices or SOA

Let's talk prerequisites. I assume that you
have a good understanding of Java and

particularly Java 8, as well as a good understanding of Spring Boot as Spring Cloud is largely built on top of Spring Boot. Last, I expect that you have at least a knowledge or an understanding of microservices or service-oriented architectures.

Java 8+

Maven 3+

Spring Tool Suite (Eclipse STS) 3.8+

Next, let's talk about what software you're going to need to be successful in this book. Of course you're going to need Java, Java 8, and you'll need Maven, at least Maven 3, in order to build the Spring Boot applications. And we're going to be doing all of our development using Spring Tool Suite, or Eclipse STS, as it's called. Make sure you have at least version 3.8.

Module 3: Finding Services Using Service Discovery

What Is Service Discovery?

- **In this module :**
  - **Service Discovery**
  - **Discovering Services with Spring Cloud**
    - **Using Eureka client and server**
    - **Configuration**
    - **Health & High Availability**

- Dashboard
- AWS Support

In this module we'll look at how service discovery helps you locate your application services in the cloud. Let's quickly start off by talking about what this module contains, and first we're going to look at service discovery. Obviously this module's about service discovery, so we'll talk about what it is and why it's important. Then, we're going to look at how Spring Cloud implements service discovery. It uses a project from Netflix that was open sourced, it's called Eureka, and we're going to talk about the Eureka Client and the Eureka Server. Then, we'll move on to configuration, configuring the Eureka Client, the Eureka Server, and the Eureka Instance and how each of those are different and what you need to do to tweak them or configure them for your needs. Then, we'll move into health and high availability. How does the Eureka Server know when your application is down or when it's unhealthy? And how do you ensure that the Eureka Server is highly available? And then we're going to look at the Eureka Dashboard, which is a nice web UI that shows you all of your registered services, how many instances there are, and whether they're up or down. And last, we're going to finish out with how Eureka has specific support for AWS. Let's get started with the most important question, what is service discovery and why do we need it? Remember that the cloud is changing the way that we build software. We're moving from building these single large applications and instead breaking them up into smaller and smaller pieces called services. And each of those individual services can then be deployed and scaled on their own, and together, as a whole, they form the overall application. And herein lies the problem. How does one service know where another service is at, its host and its port, so that it can call it and use it? For starters, we could simply configure all of our services to know the location and the port of other services that it calls. And, depending on our needs, this actually might get us pretty far. But after a while, we'll learn that there are some problems to this approach. What if, for example, you had two instances of a particular service? So, in our example here, we have Application Service A calling Application Service B. And if we used configuration, every time we added or removed a new instance of Application Service B, we'd have to update that configuration. And, well, in our example, we only have two instances. Imagine if you had hundreds of instances. The configuration management alone would be unsustainable. Our simple configuration starts to break down even further as we move to a cloud environment. In a cloud environment, you have instances of services that can come and go in response to demand, for instance. So, for example, Application Service B starts with two instances, and consider that maybe you have this huge influx of traffic, maybe it's a flash sale on your eCommerce website, and an automated process kicks off and starts two more instances to handle all of that demand. Well, if you're using simple configuration, all of the callers of Application Service B, such as Application Service A, would not even know about the two new instances that were added in response to that demand. As far as they're concerned, their configuration says that there are only two instances that they know about. Another thing to consider is that application services will eventually fail. And regardless of the situation, whether it's a memory problem or a hardware problem, if you're using simple configuration, your services are going to continue to try to send traffic to those failed instances. For example here, we have Application Service B being called by Application Service A, and it has two instances. And if one of those instances fails, Application Service A is not going to know the better, and it's going to continue to send traffic to that failed instance. We need something that is more dynamic. The simple approach is just far too static. It's too frozen in time for our needs in the cloud. That's where service discovery comes into play.

- Service discovery provides
    - A way for a service to register itself
    - A way for a service to deregister itself
    - A way for a client to find other services
    - A way to check the health of a service and remove unhealthy instances

Service discovery typically provides the following types of functionality. A way for a service to register itself. And what that means is that when a service comes online it can call out to the Service Discovery Server and let it know the location and port of its service so that other application services can call it. For the exact opposite reasons, service discovery provides a way for a service to deregister itself. So if a service were to shut down or go away temporarily for upgrades, it would want to let the Service Discovery Server know that it's no longer available for clients to use. And, most importantly, service discovery provides a way for clients to find other services. And what do I mean by clients? Well I mean other application services. So if you're an application service that needs to use another service, you need to be able to find the location and port of that service, and you can ask the Service Discovery Server for that information. Lastly, service discovery provides a way to check the health of a service and remove any unhealthy instances. So each application service would implement a health check, typically via a REST endpoint, and then the Service Discovery Server would call that endpoint. And if the health check were to fail, it would remove that instance from its registry.

Introducing Spring Cloud Netflix

Now that we have a good understanding of what service discovery is and why it's important, let's learn how Spring Cloud helps us implement it.

- Discover services with:
  - Spring Cloud Consul
  - Spring Cloud Zookeeper
  - Spring Cloud Netflix

There are actually several different ways that you can discover services using Spring Cloud. There's the Spring Cloud Consul project, there's the Spring Cloud Zookeeper project, and there's the Spring Cloud Netflix project. We're going to specifically focus on the last one, the Spring Cloud Netflix project. The folks over at Netflix have some serious experience building scalable applications in the cloud. And, in fact, you could probably even argue they have some of the largest scalability problems you can imagine. And they built some projects internally to handle these problems and eventually released them as open source projects.

- Netflix OSS + Spring + Spring Boot
    = Spring Cloud Netflix

The Spring Cloud project took the Netflix open source projects and added some Spring and some Spring Boot features. They sort of Spring-a-fide it, if you will. And what was born out of that was the Spring Cloud Netflix project. Similar to the Spring Cloud project, the Spring Cloud Netflix project is not actually a project in and of itself. Rather, it's a collection of projects. And for service discovery, we're interested in two of those projects: the Spring Cloud Netflix Eureka Server and the Spring Cloud Netflix Eureka Client.

Key Components Involved in Service Discovery

Before we dive in to the Spring Cloud Eureka Server and Client, it's helpful to understand the key components that are involved in service discovery and how they interact with each other. At a minimum, there are three components involved in service discovery. There's the Discovery Server, the application service, and the application client. It's helpful to get a full understanding of how all the components work together and from there we'll go deeper into each component and see how Spring Cloud helps us implement that particular component.

- (1) Service registers location
- (2) Client looks up service location
- (3) Discovery server sends back location
- (4) Client requests service at location
- (5) Service sends response

The first thing that happens is the application service starts up. And when it starts up, it calls out to the Discovery Server, and it registers itself. And it tells the Discovery Server its location, its port, and a service identifier that others can use to find it. Then at some point later, a client needs to call that application service, but it doesn't know the location and the port of the service, so it needs to ask the Discovery Server. It sends out a request to the Discovery Server and sends along the service identifier. And the Discovery Server knows that based on that service identifier which service you're asking for, and it responds back with the location and the port of that service. From there, things proceed as normal, and the client can request the service and its location, and the service can respond back with data.

The Discovery Server

We're going deeper with each of the key components in service discovery, and we're going to start with the Discovery Server. At its core, the Discovery Server is an actively managed registry of service locations. It is responsible for allowing others to find services and for services to register and deregister themselves. It's the source of truth, if you will. And you would typically run more than one instance of the Discovery Server as it's the key component to locate all the other services. And if you can't locate the other services, then you can't call the other services. So this is an important piece of the overall architecture. And you can find the Discovery Server implementation within the Spring Cloud Eureka Server project. Throughout the book, we're going to be doing fairly simple demos, things that are easy to set up and solidify the concepts. So in this example, we're going to learn how to create a Discovery Server using Spring Cloud. And I'll detail out each of the steps, and then we'll follow up with a real example. Creating a Discovery Server with the Spring Cloud Eureka Server project is very easy. In fact, it's almost embarrassingly easy. pom.xml :

```xml
<dependencyManagement>
   <dependencies>
     <dependency>
        <groupId>org.springframework.cloud</groupId>
        <artifactId>spring-cloud-dependencies</artifactId>
        <version>Camden.SR2</version>
        <type>pom</type>
        <scope>import</scope>
     </dependency>
   </dependencies>
</dependencyManagement>
```

In your pom.xml of your Maven project, in the dependencyManagement section, define a new dependency called spring-cloud-dependencies, and make sure it's of type pom and it has a scope of import.

```
<dependency>
        <groupId>org.springframework.cloud
</groupId>
        <artifactId>spring-cloud-starter-
eureka-server</artifactId>
</dependency>
```

Still within your pom.xml, define a new dependency, spring-cloud-starter-eureka-server. And be sure to place this within the dependency section and not within the dependencyManagement.

Application.properties :
spring.application.name=discovery-server
OR
Application.yml :
spring:application:name: discovery-server

Within your application.properties or your application.yml, define a new property, spring.application.name. And you can give this whatever value you want. In our case here, we're going to use discovery-server.

```
@SpringBootApplication
@EnableEurekaServer
public class Application{
        public static void main(String[]args){
                SpringApplication.run(Applicat
        ion.class,args);
        }
}
```

Then, in your main Application class, you literally define one annotation. It's @EnableEurekaServer. And that's all there is to it. Once you start this application up, you will having a running instance of a Discovery Server.

Demo: Setting up a Service Discovery Server

In this demo, we're going to be creating and starting up our own Service Discovery Server using the Spring Cloud Eureka Server project. To start things off, let's head over to start.spring.io, and we're going to use this Spring Initializr to create the stub for our project. It's a nice little skeleton creator that saves us a lot of time.

In the Group section here, I'm going to put io.ajay.kumar, and for the Artifact I'm going to call it the discovery-server. In the dependencies, I'm going to add the Eureka Server, this is the Discovery Server, and I'm also going to add DevTools and the Spring Boot Actuator project.

Generate a

Maven Project ▾

with

Java ▾

and Spring Boot

2.1.0 ▾

Project Metadata

Artifact coordinates

Group

io.ajay.kumar

Artifact

discovery-server

Dependencies

Add Spring Boot Starters and dependencies to your application

Search for dependencies

web, Security, JPA, Actuator, Devtools...

Selected Dependencies

Eureka Server ✕

DevTools ✕   Actuator ✕

Generate Project alt + ↵

**Once you've added all those dependencies,
click the Generate Project button. After you
click that Generate Project button, it's going
to automatically download a zip file for you,**

17

and this contains the stub of our project. Go ahead and unzip the downloaded stub project. Then we're going to go ahead and open up our IDE and import it. I've switched over to my IDE, which is Spring Tool Suite. And on the Package Explorer tab in the blank area, right-click and go to Import. And you're going to want to filter out the available options by typing in Existing Maven Projects. Go ahead and click that, click Next, browse to the location of the unzipped stub project, and click Open. Underneath the Projects you should see your pom.xml. Go ahead and click Finish, and give that a second, and it'll import into the IDE.

- ∨ 🗂 discovery-server [boot] [devtools]
  - ∨ 🗁 src/main/java
    - ∨ ⊞ io.ajay.kumar.discoveryserver
      - › 🗋 DiscoveryServerApplication.java
  - ∨ 🗁 src/main/resources
    - 🖉 application.properties
  - ∨ 🗁 src/test/java
    - ∨ ⊞ io.ajay.kumar.discoveryserver
      - › 🗋 DiscoveryServerApplicationTests.java
  - › ➡️ JRE System Library [JavaSE-1.8]
  - › ➡️ Maven Dependencies
  - › 🗁 src
  - 🗁 target
  - 📄 mvnw
  - 🗋 mvnw.cmd
  - 🗋 pom.xml

Once the project is finished importing, go ahead and expand it and open up the main application class. It should be called DiscoveryServerApplication, and this is where we're going to add the annotation to enable our Discovery Server. So right above this @SpringBootApplication annotation, we can add a new one, @EnableEurekaServer. Go ahead and save that.

```
package io.ajay.kumar.discoveryserver;
import org.springframework.boot.SpringApplication;
import org.springframework.boot.autoconfigure.SpringBootApplication;
import org.springframework.cloud.netflix.eureka.server.EnableEurekaServer;
@EnableEurekaServer
@SpringBootApplication
public class DiscoveryServerApplication {
    public static void main(String[] args) {
        SpringApplication.run(DiscoveryServerApplication.class, args);
    }
}
```

We're now ready to start our Service Discovery Server, so go ahead and right-click on the main application class, and go to Run As, and choose Spring Boot App.

```
sport.TransportException: Cannot execute request on any known serv
shared.transport.decorator.RetryableEurekaHttpClient.execute(Retry
shared.transport.decorator.EurekaHttpClientDecorator.getApplicatio
shared.transport.decorator.EurekaHttpClientDecorator$6.execute(Eur
shared.transport.decorator.SessionedEurekaHttpClient.execute(Sessi
shared.transport.decorator.EurekaHttpClientDecorator.getApplicatio
DiscoveryClient.getAndStoreFullRegistry(DiscoveryClient.java:1051)
```

Once the application has finished loading, go ahead and expand the Console widow. And you'll notice that there are several exceptions in here. Go ahead and stop the application server; otherwise, it will continue to throw those exceptions. Let's scroll up to one of these exceptions and see what the problem is. Cannot execute request on any known server. And if you look, it's coming from this DiscoveryClient.getAndStoreFullRegistry method. And what's happening is the Service Discovery Server is starting up, and it's trying to register itself with a peer Service Discovery Server. And this is mainly for high availability purposes. However, when we're running in standalone or development mode, it can kind of be a pain to have to set up multiple instances every time. So instead, we're going to configure the Eureka Server not to try to register itself with its peers. And you definitely only want to do this is development mode since you want that high availability in production. Let's go ahead and close the Console. Then, in the Package Explorer, navigate to src/main/resources and open up the application.properties.

application.properties :
spring.application.name=discovery-server
eureka.client.register-with-eureka=false
eureka.client.fetch-registry=false
server.port=8761

The first property we're going to add is actually one that we forgot previously, it's the spring.application.name property, and we're going to set that to discovery-server. The second property we're going to add is a Eureka Client property, so go ahead and type eureka.client.register-with-eureka. And since we're the Discovery Server our self, and we're running in standalone mode, we don't need to register with any other peers because there aren't any other peers. So make sure you set that value to false. The next property is also a Eureka Client property, so go ahead and type eureka.client.fetch-registry. And this property controls whether or not the Eureka Client would fetch the registry from the Eureka Server, and since we are the only Eureka Server, there's nothing else to fetch from

20

anybody else, so we'll set this to false. And the last property we're going to add is the server.port, and we're going to set that to a value of 8761, which is the default port for Eureka Discovery Server. Once you get those properties in place, head over to the main application class, right-click on it, and go to Run As Spring Boot App. When your app finishes starting up, expand the console, and you'll see that it started the Eureka Server and it changed its status to UP. So you now have a running Service Discovery Server.

The Application Service

- **Provides some application functionality**
- **The receiver of requests**
- **A dependency of other service(s)**
- **One or more instances**
- **User of the discovery client**
  - **Register**
  - **Deregister**

Remember that we're diving into each of the components of service discovery, and the next on our list is the application service. This is whatever is providing the functionality. It's the thing that's receiving the requests from clients and returning responses. And it's a dependency of other services. So other services depend on its functionality to perform their functionality. You would typically run one or more instances of the application service. The application service is a user of the discovery client. It's going to use that client to call out to the Discovery Server and register and deregister itself. Just like we did for the Service Discovery Server, we're going to detail out the steps needed to add a Eureka Client to an application service, and then we'll actually create one ourselves.

- **Using Spring Cloud Eureka Client in a Service**

pom.xml :

```xml
<dependencyManagement>
  <dependencies>
    <dependency>
      <groupId>org.springframework.cloud</groupId>
      <artifactId>spring-cloud-dependencies</artifactId>
      <version>Camden.SR2</version>
      <type>pom</type>
      <scope>import</scope>
    </dependency>
  </dependencies>
</dependencyManagement>
```

In the pom.xml of your Maven project, add a new dependencyManagement section, and within there add a new dependency of spring-cloud-dependencies. Again, make sure it's of type pom and of scope import.

pom.xml:

```xml
<dependency>
<groupId>org.springframework.cloud</groupId>
<artifactId>spring-cloud-starter-eureka</artifactId>
</dependency>
```

Still within the pom.xml, add a new dependency within the dependencies elements, and this one is called spring-cloud-starter-eureka. Then in your application.properties or your application.yml, add two new properties.

application.properties

spring.application.name=service

eureka.client.service-
url.defaultZone=http://localhost:8761/eureka
OR
application.yml
spring:application:name: service
eureka:client:service-url:defaultZone:
http://localhost:8761/eureka
The first property is the
spring.application.name property, and again
you can set this to whatever value you want.
In our case, we'll use service. The second
property tells the application service where
the Service Discovery Server is located, and
it's the eureka.client.defaultZone property.
And you can see we set that to localhost, but in
a production configuration you'd obviously set
that to wherever your Service Discovery
Server was located. If you're wondering what
the defaultZone piece is of the property, don't
worry about it for now. We'll explain more
about that in the AWS support section.

```
@SpringBootApplication
@EnableDiscoveryClient
publicclassApplication{
publicstaticvoidmain(String[]args){
SpringApplication.run(Application.class,args)
;
}
}
```

And then in your main Application class of
your application service, you add one
annotation. Again, it's just one annotation.
The Spring Cloud guys have made it so easy
for us. And that is the
@EnableDiscoveryClient annotation. And
what this does is it makes our application
service register itself with the Discovery
Server, and then other services can find it.

Demo: Making an Application Service Discoverable

We'll use the Spring Initializr again to create our application service, so go ahead and head over to start.spring.io. And in the Group here you're going to put io.ajay.kumar, and we'll give the Artifact name service. And you'll have pretty much the same dependencies, but this time you'll want to do the Eureka Discovery dependency instead of the Eureka Server dependency. And you can go ahead and add DevTools and the Actuator.

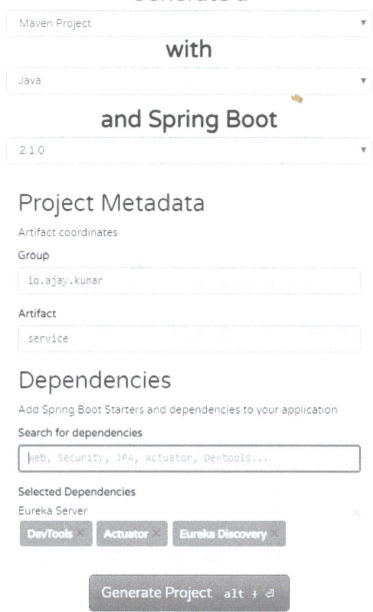

Generate a

Maven Project ▾

with

Java ▾

and Spring Boot

2.1.0 ▾

Project Metadata

Artifact coordinates

Group

io.ajay.kumar

Artifact

service

Dependencies

Add Spring Boot Starters and dependencies to your application

Search for dependencies

Web, Security, JPA, Actuator, Devtools...

Selected Dependencies

Eureka Server ✕

DevTools ✕   Actuator ✕   Eureka Discovery ✕

Generate Project   alt + ↵

**Go ahead and click Generate Project. It'll
automatically create and download a zip file
for you. Go ahead and unzip that zip file, and
we'll import that into our IDE. And we're**

back in Spring Tool Suite. In the Package
Explorer tab, right-click and go to Import.
And again, we want to do Existing Maven
Projects. Click Next, browse to the location of
our unzipped file, and click Open. You should
see the pom.xml underneath the Projects
heading, and click Finish to finish the import.
That'll take a second, and once that's finished,
expand the service and go to src/main/java
and open up the main application class.

- service [boot] [devtools]
  - src/main/java
    - io.ajay.kumar.service
      - ServiceApplication.java
  - src/main/resources
    - application.properties
  - src/test/java
    - io.ajay.kumar.service
      - ServiceApplicationTests.java
  - JRE System Library [JavaSE-1.8]
  - Maven Dependencies
  - src
  - target
  - mvnw
  - mvnw.cmd
  - pom.xml

package io.ajay.kumar.service;
import
org.springframework.beans.factory.annotatio
n.Value;
import
org.springframework.boot.SpringApplication;
import
org.springframework.boot.autoconfigure.Spri
ngBootApplication;
import
org.springframework.cloud.client.discovery.E
nableDiscoveryClient;

```java
import
org.springframework.web.bind.annotation.Re
questMapping;
import
org.springframework.web.bind.annotation.Re
stController;
@EnableDiscoveryClient
@SpringBootApplication
@RestController
public class ServiceApplication {
    @Value("${service.instance.name}")
    private String instance;
    public static void main(String[] args) {
        SpringApplication.run(ServiceAppli
cation.class, args);
    }

    @RequestMapping("/")
    public String message() {
        return "Hello from " + instance;
    }
}
```

Within the main application class, called
ServiceApplication, we'll add
@EnableDiscoveryClient. And this is what's
going to turn our service application into a
client of the Discovery Server, and it's going to
cause it to register with the Discovery Server
when it starts up. Underneath the
SpringBootApplication annotation, add a new
annotation, @RestController. And remember
that we're doing quick and easy demos to
solidify the concepts, and some of the things
that we're using here are definitely not best
practices, and you shouldn't use them in your
regular applications. So, for instance, you
wouldn't typically put an @RestController on
your main application class, but since we're
using this to quickly demo something, it's

okay. Let's add a new method here, public String message. And we're going to return a message. And we're going to want to annotate this with @RequestMapping, and we'll just make this the root. And the plan is to be able to start multiple instances of this service application. So we're going to add a property here called private String instance. And we're going to annotate this with @Value, and we're going to pass in a placeholder of service.instance.name. Go ahead and save that, and then in your message return "Hello from " + instance;.

application.properties
spring.application.name=service
eureka.client.service-url.defaultZone=http://localhost:8761/eureka
Under src/main/resources, open up the application.properties and give this a spring.application.name. And we'll call this service. And we're going to add one more property, and that's the location of the Discovery Server. So you can type eureka.client.service-url. And after the service-url, you typically put a zone, and there's a default zone which we'll use. It's called defaultZone. And then we're going to set that to the location of our Service Discovery Server, so http://localhost:8761/eureka. Since we're going to be running more than one instance of our service application, we have to set up some run configuration so that each instance runs on a different port and has a different instance name. Right-click on your main service application class, go to Run As, and go to Run Configurations. Highlight the Spring Boot App section and click New. And under Project we're going to do service, and under Main

28

type we're going to do
io.ajay.kumar.ServiceApplication. And under
the Override properties section, we're going to
add server.port, and were going to give this a
value of 8081. And then we're also going to
name our instance, so service.instance.name.
That's the property that we came up with.
And we'll call this instance 1. And don't forget
to name your instance, so we'll call this
instance 1.

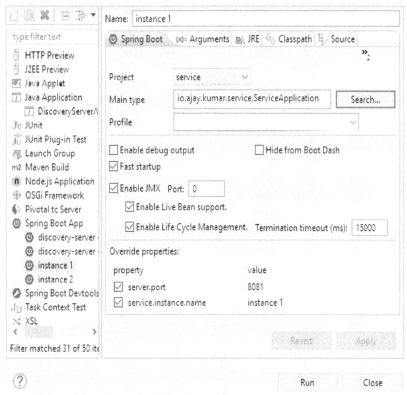

And then we're going to copy this run
configuration to create our second instance. So
if you come over here to the Duplicate button,
click that, give it a new name of instance 2.
We're going to change the port to 8082 and
the instance to 2. Click Apply, and close that.
Before we start the instances of our service

application, we need to start the Discovery Server so they can register themselves. So go ahead and expand the discovery-server, right-click on the main application class, and go to Run As Spring Boot App. Once the Service Discovery Server is started up, we can start up our application instances. So come down to the main ServiceApplication class, right-click, Run As, and go to the Run Configurations. Highlight instance 1 and click Run. And you can do the same thing for instance 2. So right-click on the ServiceApplication, Run As, Run Configurations, highlight instance 2, and click Run. You can look at each of the instances by clicking this drop-down over here. And you can see that we have the discovery-server started, the instance 1 started, and instance 2 started. And we're currently looking at instance 2. So if we expand out the Console, scroll over, and we can see that our application successfully registered itself with the Discovery Server. It says registering service, and it has a registration status of 204. DiscoveryClient_SERVICE/DESKTOP-OIHU6JB:service:8082: registering service... DiscoveryClient_SERVICE/DESKTOP-OIHU6JB:service:8082 - registration status: 204

And we can go look at the other instance, instance 1, scroll over, and we can see the same thing, registering service and a registration status of 204. DiscoveryClient_SERVICE/DESKTOP-OIHU6JB:service:8081: registering service... Tomcat started on port(s): 8081 (http) with context path ''
Updating port to 8081
Started ServiceApplication in 7.717 seconds (JVM running for 8.896)

DiscoveryClient_SERVICE/DESKTOP-OIHU6JB:service:8081 - registration status: 204

And then if you go look at the discovery-server, and you'll see several requests in there for our service application to register itself with the Service Discovery Server.

Registered instance SERVICE/DESKTOP-OIHU6JB:service:8081 with status UP (replication=false)

Registered instance SERVICE/DESKTOP-OIHU6JB:service:8081 with status UP (replication=true)

Running the evict task with compensationTime 11ms

Registered instance SERVICE/DESKTOP-OIHU6JB:service:8082 with status UP (replication=false)

Registered instance SERVICE/DESKTOP-OIHU6JB:service:8082 with status UP (replication=true)

The Application Client

- Calls another application service to implement its functionality
- The issuer of requests
- Depends on other service(s)
- User of the discovery client
  - Find service locations

Let's continue with our deep dive of the components involved in service discovery. Up next is the application client. The application client is the piece that would call out to another application service to implement some piece of functionality in its service. It's the issuer of requests, and it depends on other services. And similar to the application service, the application client is also a user of the discovery client, but it uses the discovery client in a different way. It doesn't use it to register or deregister anything. It uses it to find service locations. Just to be clear, it's perfectly reasonable for an application to be both a service and a client. An application can be a service, which provides services to others, and at the same time can be a client, which depends on other services. What we're referring to here is if the application was just a client and it wasn't a service. The steps involved to set up a client are quite similar to the steps involved to set up a service.

- **Using Spring Cloud Eureka Client in an Application Client**

pom.xml :

```
<dependencyManagement>
  <dependencies>
    <dependency>
      <groupId>org.springframework.cloud</groupId>
      <artifactId>spring-cloud-dependencies</artifactId>
      <version>Camden.SR2</version>
      <type>pom</type>
      <scope>import</scope>
    </dependency>
  </dependencies>
</dependencyManagement>
```

You add this dependencyManagement section with the spring-cloud-dependencies, and you add a dependency for spring-cloud-starter-eureka.

```
<dependency>
<groupId>org.springframework.cloud</groupId>
```

```
<artifactId>spring-cloud-starter-eureka</artifactId>
</dependency>
```

The differences between an application client and an application service come in the configuration.

application.properties

```
spring.application.name=client
eureka.client.service-url.defaultZone=http://localhost:8761/eureka
eureka.client.register-with-eureka=false
```

OR

application.yml

```
spring:application:name: client
eureka:client:service-url:defaultZone: http://localhost:8761/eureka
register-with-eureka: false
```

We have the same two properties that we used within the application service, the spring.application.name, except this time we set it to client, and the eureka.client.defaultZone so that it can know the location of the Service Discovery Server. And since we're a client, we're not interested in registering with the Discovery Server because we don't need anybody to discover us. We're just interested in discovering others. So you set that value to false.

```
@SpringBootApplication
@EnableDiscoveryClient
public class Application{
	public static void main(String[]args){
		SpringApplication.run(Application.class,args);
	}
}
```

Just like we did with the application service, we'll add the @EnableDiscoveryClient annotation to our main Application class in our application client. And then to actually discover services, we have two different options.

- @Inject EurekaClientclient
- @Inject DiscoveryClientclient

We can inject the EurekaClient or we can inject the DiscoveryClient. And just to be clear, this is the Spring DiscoveryClient and not the Netflix DiscoveryClient.

InstanceInfo instance=eurekaClient.getNextServerFromEureka(
"service-id",false);
String baseUrl = instance.getHomePageUrl();

The first option is using the EurekaClient, and the EurekaClient has a method, getNextServerFromEureka. And that'll pick the next instance in a round-robin fashion from the Discovery Server. And its first argument is a virtual host name or a service ID to call. And this is the same as the spring.application.name property that we've used in our service application. And the second argument is whether or not this is a secure request. Once we get a reference to the instance info, we can call instance.getHomePageUrl, and that'll give us the base URL that we can use with our RestTemplate to call the service.

List<ServiceInstance> instances=client.getInstances("service-id");
String baseUrl=instances.get(0).getUri().toString();

The second option is to use the Spring DiscoveryClient, and it has a method called getInstances, which returns you all service instances for a given service ID. So that first argument is the same first argument that we saw in the EurekaClient, which is a virtual hostname or a service ID of the service you want to call. And once you have a list of instances, you can get one of those instances, and you can get the URI, turn it into a string, and that's your base URL that you would use in your RestTemplate.

Demo: Finding and Calling Services as an Application Client

In order to create our client, we're going to again start off at start.spring.io. And we're going to give it a group ID, the same one, so io.ajay.kumar, and we'll make the Artifact client. And it will have the exact same dependencies that we used in the application service. So we want Eureka Discovery, want DevTools, and we want the Actuator.

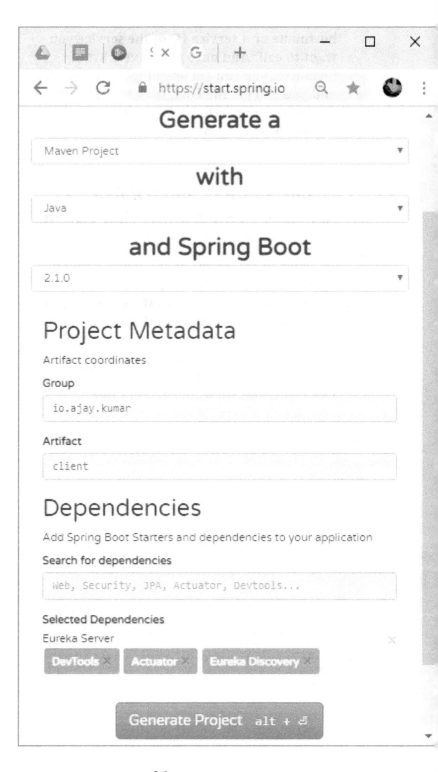

Click Generate Project. That'll automatically create and download a zip file. Go ahead and unzip that file, and we'll import that into our IDE. Within Spring Tool Suite in the Package Explorer area, right-click in the empty area, go to Import, choose Existing Maven Projects, browse to the location of your unzipped file, ensure that the pom.xml shows up under the Projects heading, and click Finish to import.

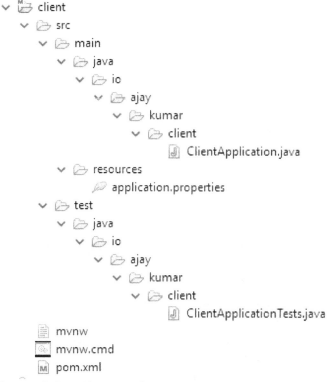

Expand the client project, and go to src/main/java, and open up the main application class and do the following changes.
package io.ajay.kumar.client;
import org.springframework.beans.factory.annotation.Autowired;
import org.springframework.boot.SpringApplication;

```java
import
org.springframework.boot.autoconfigure.Spri
ngBootApplication;
import
org.springframework.boot.web.client.RestTe
mplateBuilder;
import
org.springframework.cloud.client.discovery.E
nableDiscoveryClient;
import
org.springframework.http.HttpMethod;
import
org.springframework.http.ResponseEntity;
import
org.springframework.web.bind.annotation.Re
questMapping;
import
org.springframework.web.bind.annotation.Re
stController;
import
org.springframework.web.client.RestTemplat
e;
import com.netflix.appinfo.InstanceInfo;
import com.netflix.discovery.EurekaClient;
@EnableDiscoveryClient
@SpringBootApplication
@RestController
public class ClientApplication {
    @Autowired
    private EurekaClient client;

    @Autowired
    private RestTemplateBuilder
restTemplateBuilder;
    public static void main(String[] args) {
        SpringApplication.run(ClientApplic
ation.class, args);
    }
```

```
@RequestMapping("/")
public String callService() {
        RestTemplate restTemplate =
restTemplateBuilder.build();
        InstanceInfo instanceInfo =
client.getNextServerFromEureka("service",
false);
        String baseUrl =
instanceInfo.getHomePageUrl();
        ResponseEntity<String> response =
                restTemplate.exchange(bas
eUrl, HttpMethod.GET, null, String.class);
        return response.getBody();
    }
}
```

In the main application class, add a new annotation, @EnableDiscoveryClient. We'll also add a @RestController annotation, and we'll add a handler method, public String callService. And we'll give this an @RequestMapping, and we'll map this to root. Then we'll want to autowire in our DiscoveryClient or our EurekaClient. We'll use the EurekaClient, so private EurekaClient. We'll call it client. And we'll use @Autowired. You can also use @Inject. And we'll also need a RestTemplate so we can actually call the service, so we'll say private RestTemplateBuilder, and we'll call this a restTemplateBuilder. We will autowire that as well. And within our callService method, we'll create a new RestTemplate using the RestTemplateBuilder, so RestTemplate restTemplate = restTemplateBuilder.build. And then we're going to use the client to fetch our service URLs, so client.getNextServerFromEureka. And the virtualHostname, remember we called our spring.application.name of our service. We

just called it service. And it's going to be a
non-secure request, so put false. And this
returns an InstanceInfo, which we'll call
instanceInfo. And then we can get the base
URL and call the RestTemplate, so String
baseUrl = instanceInfo.getHomePageUrl. And
then we'll use the RestTemplate to call the
service. So the RestTemplate returns
ResponseEntity of String. We'll call that
response, and we'll say
restTemplate.exchange. And we'll pass at the
baseUrl and HttpMethod of GET. We don't
have any request bodies, so we'll do the
requestEntity as null, the responseType as
String, and we don't have any uriVariables
either, so we'll just get rid of that parameter.
And let's just go over this again before we
finish up here. So the EurekaClient is calling
out to the Discovery Server, and it's getting
information about a service ID called service,
and it's returning it back to us as an
instanceInfo. And then from that instanceInfo,
we're getting the HomePageUrl, which is the
base URL of our service, and then we're using
our restTemplate to call that service,
specifically a GET on that service, and it
returns a string back to us. And then we're
just going to return that response, so
response.getBody.
application.properties :
spring.application.name=client
eureka.client.service-
url.defaultZone=http://localhost:8761/eureka
eureka.client.register-with-eureka=false
Next, we need to configure our application
client. So head over to the src/main/resources
and open up the application.properties, and
we'll add the standard
spring.application.name. We'll call this client.

And then we're going to paste in the service URL so we don't have to type it, and then we're going to do eureka.client.register-with-eureka. We're going to set that to false. Remember, we're a client, and we don't need to register with Eureka because we don't need anybody to discover us. Now, before we start our application client, we need to start the Discovery Server and each of the application service instances, and in that particular order. So, if you've been following along, those should be in your run history. So you can come up to drop-down and choose each of those to start those up. And just to confirm, we'll check the drop-down, and we can see that we have the discovery-server running, and instance 1 of the service application, and instance 2. So now we're ready to start our client application. We can right-click on the main application class, go to Run As, and choose Spring Boot App.

Hello from instance 1

Fire up a web browser and visit localhost:8080. Hit Enter, and you should see a response from the client. And it'll say Hello from instance 1. And if you refresh it, it'll say Hello from instance 2. And we can continue to do that over and over, and each time we can see that it's getting a different instance from the Eureka registry.

Spring Cloud Eureka Dashboard

One of the really useful things that the Spring Cloud Eureka Server provides is a dashboard. It's enabled by default, and it's a web-based dashboard. And it displays a bunch of useful information, like whether or not a service is up or down and how many instances of it are registered. If you still have the demo running from our last demo, fire up a browser and visit localhost:8761. You'll be presented with this Spring Eureka Dashboard, and let's go through each of these sections here.

System Status

Environment	test
Data center	default

Current time	2018-11-22T22:32:37 +0530
Uptime	4 days 04:04
Lease expiration enabled	true
Renews threshold	5
Renews (last min)	8

DS Replicas

localhost

Instances currently registered with Eureka

Application	AMIs	Availability Zones	Status
SERVICE	n/a (2)	(2)	UP (2) - DESKTOP-OIHU6JB:service:8082 , DESKTOP-OIHU6JB:service:8081

General Info

Name	Value
total-avail-memory	329mb
environment	test
num-of-cpus	4
current-memory-usage	250mb (75%)
server-uptime	4 days 04:04
registered-replicas	http://localhost:8761/eureka/
unavailable-replicas	http://localhost:8761/eureka/,
available-replicas	

Instance Info

Name	Value
ipAddr	192.168.29.2
status	UP

So first we have the System Status, and it tells you things like the current time, the uptime, and how many renewals have happened in the last minute. The DS Replicas, or the Discovery Server Replica section, shows you all of the peer instances of Eureka Servers. So if we had more than one instance running, we would see each of those instances listed here. But since we've only got one instance, we just see localhost. The next section is probably the most useful section as it shows you what instances are currently registered with Eureka. And we have here the service ID under the Application heading, which is SERVICE. AMI is for Amazon Machine Image. We're not running in Amazon, so that's n/a. And Availability Zones, there are two, and both of those instances are UP. You can see the 2 next to the UP, which indicates that there are two instances of this particular service, and both of them are UP. And right next to that you can see both of those instances, one of them running on 8082 and one of them running on 8081. The next section, the General Info section, just gives you information about the particular machine that you're running on. So it tells you things like the number of CPUs and the available memory. And the last part, the Instance Info, gives you information about this particular running instance, so things like its IP address or whether or not it's up or down.

Configuration

There are several different areas where you can configure Spring Cloud Eureka. We'll take a look at the three main areas. The first is the eureka.server prefix, the second is the eureka.client prefix, and the third is the eureka.instance prefix. Let's go into more detail into each of these areas of configuration. The first one is the Eureka Server Configuration, and that's all configuration under the eureka.server prefix. And this is going to control everything that's related to configuring the Discovery Server. The second one is the Eureka Client Configuration, and that's all configuration under the eureka.client prefix. And this is responsible for controlling how the discovery client interacts with the Discovery Server. So for instance, you have things like the eureka.client.eureka-server-connect-timeout-seconds. This would control how long the client waits to connect to the Eureka Server before it times out. The third area of configuration is the Eureka Instance, and that's all configuration under the eureka.instance prefix. And a Eureka Instance is anything that registers itself with the Eureka Server so that it can be discovered by others. The properties under the eureka.instance prefix control how the instance registers itself with the Eureka Server. So for instance, you have things like the eureka.hostname or the eureka.health-check-url, and the instance could be configured with custom values there, and that's how it would register with the Eureka Server.

Health and High Availability

The Spring Cloud Eureka Server also has some additional features around health and high availability. It's constantly ensuring that the application services that it's returning or handing back to clients are healthy and available. And it also ensures that in the event that the Discovery Server goes down, all clients can still continue to operate. Like I mentioned, the Eureka Server is constantly concerned with the health of the application services that it's handing out to clients. And it assesses that health, at least by default, by sending the clients a heartbeat every 30 seconds. And if it doesn't hear back from that heartbeat after 90 seconds, it removes it from the registry. Sending a heartbeat is the default configuration, but you can also configure the Eureka Server to hit an endpoint, such as the /health endpoint that comes with Spring Boot Actuator. Eureka was built with high availability in mind, and one of the ways that it achieves that is when a client requests a service location from the Discovery Server, the Discovery Server actually sends back a copy of the registry. And what ends up happening is the registry gets distributed across all of the clients. And if the Service Discovery Server goes down, those clients can continue to operate. You're probably thinking well wait though. What if the Discovery Server has new information or one of the services goes down? Well, the client has to renew its lease or fetch a new registry every so often, and it does so by fetching deltas to update its registry. So it's pretty smart about not fetching the full registry again and only getting the changes.

AWS Support

It's well known that Netflix is a heavy user of AWS. And given that Eureka was born at Netflix, it's only fitting that it includes AWS support. Let's take a look at the various support, as well as a typical deployment architecture. When an application that's using the Eureka Client starts up, it checks to see if it's running on an AWS instance. If it is, it calls out to the local metadata service and retrieves some metadata about that instance. And it gets things that are specific to AWS, such as the Amazon Machine Image that's running or what region it's running in or what zone. And then it sends that information up to the Discovery Server when it registers. Given the fact that things can change so often in AWS, it's important that the Discovery Server be located at a well-known location. So Eureka adds support for Elastic IP binding. When a Eureka Server starts up and it notices that it's running in AWS, it'll try to bind to the next available Elastic IP so that it has a static or well-known IP. The Eureka Client is also zone aware with a preference for the zone that it's currently running in. So it'll try to contact the Discovery Server in its current zone, and if it can't reach one, it'll try the next zone and try to find the next available Discovery Server. And last, you can configure the Eureka Client to fetch the registry of different remote regions. In order to utilize the AWS support, it requires a little bit of extra configuration.

```
@Configuration
public class AppConfig{
        @Bean
        public EurekaInstanceConfigBean
        eurekaInstanceConfig(
        InetUtilsProperties properties){
                EurekaInstanceConfigBean
                bean=new
                EurekaInstanceConfigBean(new
                InetUtils(
                properties));
                AmazonInfo info=
                AmazonInfo.Builder.newBuilde
                r().autoBuild(
                "eureka");
```

```
            bean.setDataCenterInfo(info);
            return bean;
      }
}
```

In your @Configuration class, you define a new method that returns a EurekaInstanceConfigBean, and you annotate that with @Bean. And within the method, you create a new EurekaInstanceConfigBean. Then you create an AmazonInfo object using the AmazonInfo.Builder, and you set the DataCenterInfo on the EurekaInstanceConfigBean to that AmazonInfo and then return that bean. If you were to go and look at the source of the AmazonInfo class, you would see that it's utilizing the local metadata service to fill in all of the instance information. In addition to the configuration in your @Configuration class, there's also some additional configuration in your application.properties, and that's around configuring the availability zones.

- Availability Zones Configuration in application.properties
  - eureka.client.availability-zones.[region]=[az1],[az2],[az3]

The property is the eureka.client.availability-zones property, and the pattern is eureka.client.availability-zones.region, and then that's equal to a comma-separated list of availability zones.

EC2 Dashboard :

Name	Instance ID	Instance Type	Availability Zone
spring-cloud-discovery-server-1	i-782b7576	t2.micro	us-east-1b
spring-cloud-discovery-server-2	i-b9bcba41	t2.micro	us-east-1e

So for example, if you have the following where you have one Discovery Server in the us-east-1b zone and another Discovery Server

49

in the us-east-1e zone, you would set up your property as follows: eureka.client.availability-zones, and then the region is us-east-1, and then you would set the comma-separated list of us-east-1b and us-east-1e. Similar configuration is required in the application.properties for your service URLs.

- Service URL Configuration in application.properties
  - eureka.client.service-url.[zone]=http://[eip-dns]/eureka

The property is the eureka.client.service-url.zone property, and you set that to the HTTP address of the Eureka Instance that's bound to an Elastic IP. And you want to make sure, at least as of version 1.4, to use the Elastic IP DNS name as the code is specifically aware of the pattern that Elastic IPs use for DNS names, and it's looking for that specific pattern to recognize if it's using an Elastic IP. Elastic IP Dashboard :

Address	▲	Allocation ID	▼	Instance ID	▼	Network Interface ID
34.192.167.121		eipalloc-bdf9e782		i-782b7576		eni-2d3231d2
34.193.24.166		eipalloc-59e3fd66		i-b9bcba41		eni-f1e0c418

If, for instance, we had the following Elastic IPs allocated to us, we could configure our application.properties as follows: with the first one being the us-east-1b zone and then second one being the us-east-1e zone. And if you'll notice, each of those is set to the Elastic IP DNS name for the HTTP address. Following along with the previous screenshots of the AWS console and how we configured everything, if you were to load up your Eureka Dashboard after setting all of that up, it would look like this.

DS Replicas

ec2-34-192-167-121.compute-1.amazonaws.com

ec2-34-193-24-166.compute-1.amazonaws.com

Instances currently registered with Eureka

Application	AMIs	Availability Zones	Status
DISCOVERY-SERVER-1	ami-40d28157 (1)	us-east-1b (1)	UP (1) - i-782b7576
DISCOVERY-SERVER-2	ami-40d28157 (1)	us-east-1e (1)	UP (1) - i-b9bcba41

You would have two instances under your DS Replicas, and then you would have two instances of Discovery Servers, each in their respective availability zones.

Instance Info

Name	Value
public-ipv4	34.192.167.121
public-hostname	ec2-34-192-167-121.compute-1.amazonaws.com
instance-id	i-782b7576
instance-type	t2.micro
ami-id	ami-40d28157
ipAddr	172.31.52.243
status	UP
availability-zone	us-east-1b

Likewise, you'd be able to pull up the dashboard on each of those Discovery Server instances, and you'd find AWS-specific metadata filled in, like the instance-type or the ami-id or the instance-id.

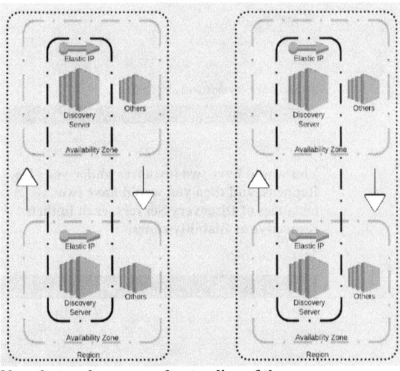

Now that we have an understanding of the AWS support that exists in Eureka, let's take a look at a deployment architecture. Typically you would have one or more Discovery Servers per each availability zone, and then you'd have multiple availability zones. And within each of those zones, you would have one Elastic IP for each of the Discovery Servers. Then you would typically have an auto scaling group set up that evenly distributes those Discovery Servers across the availability zones.

Summary

We've reached the end of this module, so let's quickly go over what we learned. We started off by taking a look at what service discovery is and why it's important. Then we learned how to use the Spring Cloud Eureka Client to discover services and the Spring Cloud Eureka Server to store a registry of services so that others could discover them. Then we took a quick look at the Spring Cloud Eureka Dashboard and saw an insight into the Spring Cloud Eureka Server. From there, we talked about health checks, high availability, and configuring Spring Cloud Eureka. And we finished off by looking at the AWS specific support.

Module 4: Configuring Services Using Distributed Configuration

What Is a Configuration Server?

In this module we'll talk about managing your application configuration in a distributed system like the cloud. We'll jump right in with configuration in a distributed system and why its different and more challenging than a non-distributed system, and more importantly, why we need this thing called a Configuration Server. From there, we'll dive into the details behind the way Spring Cloud Implements a Configuration Server with the Spring Cloud Config Server. And we'll see how you can set up a Config Client and a Config Server and get them talking to each other. We'll also quickly go over the various back-end storing options for Spring Cloud Config Server, such as a Git repository or an SVN repository. Next, and one of the things that I think is the coolest, we'll learn how to update our configuration on the fly without ever restarting our application server. And we'll do that with a variety of methods including the Spring Cloud Actuator, Spring Cloud Bus, and the Spring Cloud Monitor projects. Then we'll also learn about the @RefreshScope annotation and why it's needed and where to use it. We'll finish out the module on a section about retrieving and storing your sensitive configuration values using symmetric and asymmetric encryption. So, what exactly is so different about managing the configuration in a cloud-native application versus a non-cloud-native application? The answer to that stems from the fact that a cloud-native application is a distributed system and non-cloud-native applications are not distributed. And in a non-distributed application, you typically only have a handful of configuration files. It's often a one-to-one relationship between a system and its configuration. And as you move to a distributed system, that configuration explodes. You go from having one or more to many, many configuration files because you have many, many systems that make up one system as a whole. For instance, if you're using microservices, each one of your individual microservices that composed your overall application would have its own configuration file. You might be thinking no problem. We've got this. That's why they make configuration tools like Puppet and Chef for managing configuration in many, many systems, right? Well, it'll work, but it's not ideal for the cloud. Let's talk about some of the issues that you would face with using a typical configuration management system. The first is that it's typically deployment oriented. And that means that any time you want to make a configuration change, you have to kick off a new deployment so that the configuration is modified. And typically the application is then usually restarted. What if, for instance, you needed to make a temporary logging configuration change to debug an issue? Kicking off a whole new deployment and restarting applications is a pretty heavy process just for a temporary change. Another issue that you would encounter is the way in which configuration changes make it to the application servers. And that's via a push. Pushing application configuration to servers in a cloud environment is usually not dynamic enough. And by that, I mean it needs to know where to push the configuration to. And in the cloud that's usually not a straightforward answer as application instances can come and go at any given point in time. When you push configuration, you run the risk of missing a newly started instance that, for instance, came online as a result of auto scaling during a high-traffic period. Okay, so no problem. If push doesn't work, we can just use pull, right? Well, that has problems too. When you pull configuration, you typically use a pulling mechanism where you check for changes every x number of minutes, and if there are changes, then you pull those changes down. And that introduces latency from the time that we change our configuration to the time that it actually takes effect. Well, if configuration management tooling doesn't solve our problem, then what exactly does? The answer to that is something called a Configuration Server. Or, to be more specific, an Application Configuration Server. An Application Configuration Server is a dedicated, dynamic, and centralized key/value store for storing your configuration. And it could be distributed or non-distributed. And similar to configuration management, it's the authoritative source for all configuration. It provides things like auditing and versioning, and it also has cryptography support so that you can encrypt or decrypt those sensitive configuration values.

Introducing Spring Cloud Config Server

Managing your application configuration with help from Spring Cloud is really quite easy. By default, Spring Cloud provides you with several different ways to implement a Configuration Server with almost no work on your part. The first two options, Spring Cloud Consul and Spring Cloud Zookeeper, are integrations with third party applications, Consul and Zookeeper, respectively. You may or may not be familiar with Consul and Zookeeper, and in case you're not, it's important to note that neither of them is just a Configuration Server. Both are commonly utilized for other purposes like service discovery. The third option, Spring Cloud Config Server, is an implementation that was built by the Spring Cloud team. And it has one sole purpose, and that's to be a Configuration Server. We'll focus specifically on this option, but it should be pretty easy to utilize the others once you have a firm understanding of the concepts. In addition to including the implementation of the Spring Cloud Config Server, the Spring Cloud Config project also includes client-side support for connecting and interacting with the server. The Config Client, which is usually imbedded in your application, fits perfectly into Spring's Environment abstraction. And that means that all the ways that you're already familiar with getting access to configuration can be used to get access to configuration that was retrieved from the Configuration Server. The Config Server is usually a standalone application, and it also fits perfectly into one of the Spring framework abstractions, and that's the PropertySource abstraction. So, if you're not familiar with the PropertySource abstraction, you've probably actually already used it. For instance, if you've ever referred to a properties file in your application using the classpath prefix, then you've already used the PropertySource abstraction. And all of the configuration that comes from the Configuration Server is just another property source. It's a property source that's remote.

Using the Spring Cloud Config Server

As we've already discussed, the Spring Cloud Config Server is an implementation of a Configuration Server. Let's take a deeper look at the functionality that it provides and how to get one set up. At its core, the Config Server is just another web application, and it provides a REST-based interface for accessing your configuration files. So you set up your configuration files, you name them appropriately, and then you tell the Configuration Server where they're located, and it'll serve them up for you. It's important to point out that the Config Server does not facilitate writing any configuration files, and it's only mainly concerned with serving those configuration files. It has support for various output formats, and the default is JSON, but it also supports properties and YAML. The Config Server doesn't need a database to store the configuration, and instead it has support for retrieving and reading your configuration files from several different back-end storage configurations like Git, which is the default, or SVN, or just the plain old filesystem. Another nice feature that the Configuration Server supports is it has some notion of configuration scopes. And what I mean by that is that you can define global configuration that applies to all applications, as well as application-specific configuration or Spring Profile specific configuration. Using the Spring Cloud Config Server, like Spring Cloud's other servers, is very, very easy.

- pom.xml:

```xml
<dependencyManagement>
  <dependencies>
    <dependency>
      <groupId>org.springframework.cloud</groupId>
      <artifactId>spring-cloud-dependencies</artifactId>
      <version>Camden.SR2</version>
      <type>pom</type>
      <scope>import</scope>
```

```
        </dependency>
    </dependencies>
</dependencyManagement>
```
First, in your pom.xml, make sure that you have the spring-cloud-dependencies defined within your dependencyManagement section.
```
<dependency>
        <groupId>org.springframework.cloud
</groupId>
        <artifactId>spring-cloud-config-
server</artifactId>
</dependency>
```
Then, still in your pom.xml, in the dependency section, define a new dependency on spring-cloud-config-server. Next, create a folder to store all of your configuration that you want the Configuration Server to serve up. And in that folder you can optionally create an application.properties file or an application.yml file. And this file is for a global configuration that should apply to all applications and not any one specific application. An example of that would be something like your database configuration that is shared across all of your applications. You would put it in this application.properties or application.yml file. Next you add application and profile-specific configuration files in this folder, and you can put them in either properties or YAML format. And you use a special naming pattern for the file name, and that's the application-profile.extension where application is the name of your application and profile is the Spring Profile that should apply for that configuration. If you're not using a Spring Profile, you can omit the -profile section of the file name and just use the application name.file extension. Next you would run git init within your folder that

contains all of your configuration files. And
this example assumes that you're using the
default back-end storage, which is Git. And
from there you would git add your
configuration files, git commit them, and then
the last step, which is optional, but highly
recommended, is to set up a remote Git
repository and git push the configuration up
to the remote repository. Now we need to
configure the actual Configuration Server
itself. Now don't confuse this with the
configuration files that the Configuration
Server will be serving. This is the application
configuration for the actual Configuration
Server.
application.properties :
server.port=8888
spring.cloud.config.server.git.uri=<uri_to_git_
repo>
OR
application.yml
server:port: 8888
spring:cloud:config:server:git:uri:
<uri_to_git_repo>
In the Config Server's application.properties
file, you specify the server.port property and
give that the value 8888. This isn't required,
but that port is the conventional port that's
used for the Configuration Server. Then you
need to configure the location of the Git
repository that contains all of the
configuration files that the server will serve.
And you do that by specifying the property
spring.cloud.config.server.git.uri, and then
you set that to the location of the Git
repository. Now if you'd uploaded that to a
remote repository, this would be the clone
URL of your repository. If you prefer to use

YAML files for your configuration, I've included the equivalent application.yml.

```
@SpringBootApplication
@EnableConfigServer
public class Application{
        public static void main(String[] args){
        SpringApplication.run(Application.class,args);
        }
}
```

The next step is to add the @EnableConfigServer annotation to your main Application class. And while you're in here, if you wanted your Configuration Server to be discoverable via service discovery, you could add the Eureka Client dependencies, configure the service discovery URL, and add the @EnableDiscoveryClient annotation, and then clients would be able to discover the Configuration Server. The last step is to ensure that your Configuration Server is set up in a secure fashion. And it's very easy to do that using the Spring Security library. And any of the methods that are supported in Spring Security are also supported in securing your Configuration Server.

Config Server REST Support: Parameters

Typically when you're interacting with the Config Server's REST endpoints, you're doing so using the Config Client; however, it's useful to understand the available endpoints, at least for debugging purposes and also if you want to use it in another language. Each of the available REST endpoints on the Config Server share a common set of parameters. And the values of those parameters influence the configuration that's returned.

- {application} maps to spring.application.name on client
- {profile} maps to spring.profiles.active on client
- {label} server side feature to refer to set of config files by name

The first parameter is the application parameter. And if you're utilizing the Spring Cloud Config Client, it uses the value from the spring.application.name property to fill in the value for that application parameter. The next parameter is the profile parameter. And again, if you're using the Spring Cloud Config Client, it's going to pull the value from the spring.profiles.active property to fill in the value for that profile parameter. So this translates into the active Spring Profile. The last parameter, the label parameter, is a feature for grouping your configuration files into kind of arbitrary named sets. And that could mean different things depending on the back-end you're using. So for instance, if you're using Git as a back-end, the label translates to the Git branch. Now take a second to look at each of these endpoint parameters, and consider them as a whole, and think about how you might combine one or two or all of them together to identify a particular configuration.

Config Server REST Support: Endpoints

By now we should have a good understanding of the purpose of each of the path-based parameters that are involved in the REST endpoints. Let's take a look at the actual REST services themselves.

- Endpoint :
  - GET/{application}/{profile}[/{label}]
- Example :
  - /myapp/dev/master
  - /myapp/prod/v2
  - /myapp/default

The first endpoint takes up to three of the parameters that we discussed with the third, the label parameter, being optional. Let's take a look at a couple of examples that can make this a bit more concrete. The first example is /myapp/dev/master. And myapp is the application name, dev is the Spring Profile, and master is the Git branch, which translates into the label. We have another example where it's slightly different than the first example. You have myapp as the application, that's the same, but you have a different profile, and that's the prod profile. And you also have a different label, which is the v2 Git branch. Now the last example is kind of important. We've got two parameters that are required, the application parameter and the profile parameter. And then that label parameter is optional. And when you use Spring and you don't set an active profile, you might not know, but it sets one for you, and it's called default. So if you were wanting to get access to the configuration that didn't apply to any particular Spring Profile, you would give it your application name and then the value default.

- Endpoint :
  - GET/{application}-{profile}.(yml| properties)
- Example :
  - /myapp-dev.yml
  - /myapp-prod.properties
  - /myapp-default.properties

The next endpoint utilizes only two of the three parameters that we discussed, the application parameter and the profile parameter. It allows you to request either YAML or properties files, and it doesn't necessarily matter what the source file is. So, for instance, if you had a source file in the YAML format, you could still request it in the properties format, and it would automatically convert it for you. The examples are very straightforward. You have something like /myapp-dev.yml or something like /myapp-prod.properties. And just like the last endpoint, you have to have a profile, so you could have something like /myapp-default.properties.

- Endpoint :
  - GET/{label}/{application}-{profile}.(yml| properties)
- Example :
  - /master/myapp-dev.yml
  - /v2/myapp-prod.properties
  - /master/myapp-default.properties

The last REST endpoint is very similar to the one we just looked at with the exception that you have to specify a label. In fact, they can be equivalent if the label you specified is master as the previous endpoint always assumes that the label is master. Just like the other examples, it's pretty straightforward. Here's an example where we have /master/myapp-dev.yml where master is the label, myapp is the application, dev is the profile, and you've chosen to use a YAML extension so you'll get it back in YAML format. And a very similar one, except this time it is a v2 for the label or the branch, the Git branch, and myapp-prod, the same application name, with prod being a different profile. And this time you've requested a properties format so it'd be returned in properties. And the last example is a lot like the first example where you have /master/myapp- and then the profile. And since the profile is a required value, remember we need to use the value default to represent that default profile, and then you're requesting it in the properties format.

Demo: Setting up a Configuration Server

In this demo, we're going to be building and starting up our own Config Server. So the easiest way to get started is to head over to start.spring.io. For the Group ID we'll use io.ajay.kumar. For the Artifact we'll use config-server. For the dependencies, we'll add the Config Server dependency, and then we'll also add the Eureka Discovery dependency. Now this is an optional dependency, but it will allow our Config Server to register itself with the Discovery Server so that Config Clients

can find it. And last, we'll use the Actuator dependency.

← → C 🔒 https://start.spring.io 🔍 ⭐

Generate a

Maven Project

with

Java

and Spring Boot

2.1.0

Project Metadata

Artifact coordinates

Group

io.ajay.kumar

Artifact

config-server

Dependencies

Add Spring Boot Starters and dependencies to your applicat

Search for dependencies

Web, Security, JPA, Actuator, Devtools...

Selected Dependencies

`Config Server ✕` `Eureka Discovery ✕` `Actuator ✕`

Generate Project alt + ⏎

Once you've got everything selected, go ahead and click Generate Project. That will create a zip file, and go ahead and unzip that, and head over to your IDE. Within Eclipse, or STS, right-click on the empty Package area, go to Import, search for Existing Maven Projects, select it, click Next, browse to the location of the downloaded zip file, so mine's in Downloads, config-server, open that, and click Finish to finish importing it.

```
v  M S  config-server [boot]
   v  (#) src/main/java
      v  (#) io.ajay.kumar.configserver
         >  J  ConfigServerApplication.java
   v  (#) src/main/resources
         application.properties
   v  (#) src/test/java
      v  (#) io.ajay.kumar.configserver
         >  J  ConfigServerApplicationTests.java
   >  JRE System Library [JavaSE-1.8]
   >  Maven Dependencies
   >  src
      target
      mvnw
      mvnw.cmd
      pom.xml
```

Expand the config-server project and navigate to the main application class.
package io.ajay.kumar.configserver;
import
org.springframework.boot.SpringApplication;
import
org.springframework.boot.autoconfigure.Spri
ngBootApplication;
import
org.springframework.cloud.config.server.Ena
bleConfigServer;
@SpringBootApplication
@EnableConfigServer

```
public class ConfigServerApplication {
    public static void main(String[] args) {
    SpringApplication.run(ConfigServerAppl
ication.class, args);
    }
}
```

 Within the main application class, add the
@EnableConfigServer annotation. Save that
and close that file. Next, expand the
src/main/resources folder and open up the
application.properties.
application.properties :
server.port=8888
spring.cloud.config.server.git.uri=
Within the application.properties, add a
server.port property and set that equal to
8888. Next, we need to configure the Config
Server to know where the configuration
repository is located. So we'll say
spring.cloud.config.server.git.uri, we're going
to use a Git repository, and then we're going
to set that to a config repository. Normally you
would set this to the location of your own
configuration repository, but for this demo
we're going to use a prebuilt one that's on
GitHub. So go ahead and open up a browser.
In the address bar, type
https://github.com/ajaycucek/config-
repository. We're going to be forking this
repository, which means we're going to be
creating a local copy in our own GitHub
account. And that requires that you have your
own GitHub account. So if you don't already,
make sure that you sign up for one. And if you
do, make sure you sign in. Once you're all
signed in, click the Fork button in the top
right corner, and that'll create a fork for you.
Once you've got your fork created, it'll look
very similar to the unforked version, but

underneath the repository name at the top it'll say forked from ajayscf-config-repository. Next we want to grab the clone URL, so head over to this green button, click it, and copy the clone URL to your clipboard, and head back over to your IDE. Back in Eclipse, or STS, we want access to the Git repository's view. And you can do that by going to Window, Show View, Other, and choose Git Repositories. Within the Git Repositories view, click on the link that says Clone a Git repository. It'll pop up a new window. Choose Clone URI. Hit Next. Since we copied it to our clipboard, it should automatically show up in the URI section with the host and the repository path filled in as well. If it's not, just pasted in that clone URL that we copied into the URI. Go ahead and click Next, choose the master branch, and click Finish.
application.properties :
server.port=8888
spring.cloud.config.server.git.uri=https://github.com/ajaycucek/config-repository.git
Since we still have the clone URL on our clipboard, let's set up the Config Server's Git URL by clicking in the application.properties and pasting in that value. Make sure you save that, and then you can close that file. Head back over to the Git Repositories view and expand the repository. Right-click on the Working Tree and choose Import Projects. A new dialog box will pop up, and just click Finish.

> ✓ ⌷ config-repository [config-repository master]
>   ⌐ application.properties
>   ⌐ config-client-app-prod.properties
>   ⌐ config-client-app.properties
>   ⌐ README.md

application.properties :

# Put all global configuration here
some.property=global
some.other.property=global
config-client-app-prod.properties :
Put application+profile-specific config here
(app name: client-config-app) (profile name:
prod)
some.property=profile specific value
some.other.property=profile specific value
config-client-app.properties :
Put application-specific config here
(application name: client-config-app)
some.property=app specific overridden value
In the Package Explorer, expand the config
repository project, and you'll notice that there
are three configuration files. Let's take a look
at the first configuration file, the
application.properties. This is where all of the
global configuration goes. The
application.properties applies to any
application that asks for configuration from
the Config Server. Next, open up the config-
client-app.properties file, and note that this is
an application-specific configuration file. So
this would only apply to an application named
config-client-app. When we demo the Spring
Cloud Config Client, we'll configure the
Spring application name of that project to be
the config-client-app so that this configuration
only applies to that application. Go ahead and
open up the last configuration file, the config-
client-app-prod.properties file. And this
configuration file is similar to the one we just
looked at. And it would apply to the same
application, but instead it would only apply to
the application if the application was running
with the Spring Profile named prod. Let's
close all of these configuration files and start
up our Configuration Server. So go over here

to the config-server, expand it, find the main application class, right-click on it, and go to Run As Spring Boot App. You need to start the discovery-server too. Once the Configuration Server is started, let's open up a browser and hit some of the REST endpoints.

← → C ⓘ localhost:8888/config-client-app/default ☆ ● ⋮

{"name":"config-client-app","profiles":
["default"],"label":null,"version":"5bbcc634f016351eecb0aaf67650c378e
9425200","state":null,"propertySources":
[{"name":"https://github.com/ajaycucek/config-repository.git/config-
client-app.properties","source":{"some.property":"app specific
overridden value"}},{"name":"https://github.com/ajaycucek/config-
repository.git/application.properties","source":
{"some.property":"global","some.other.property":"global"}]]]

Formatting above response :
```
{
  "name":"config-client-app",
  "profiles":[
    "default"
  ],
  "label":null,

  "version":"5bbcc634f016351eecb0aaf67650c3
78e9425200",
  "state":null,
  "propertySources":[
    {

  "name":"https://github.com/ajaycucek/config
-repository.git/config-client-app.properties",
      "source":{
        "some.property":"app specific
overridden value"
      }
    },
    {
```

```
      "name":"https://github.com/ajaycucek/config
-repository.git/application.properties",
      "source":{
        "some.property":"global",
        "some.other.property":"global"
      }
    }
  ]
}
```

Once you've got your browser open, visit
http://localhost:8888/config-client-app/default.
And then remember that it's the application
name/profile/label, so application name will be
config-client-app. And remember that the
profile parameter is a required parameter, so
if we want to see the default configuration for
the Config Client app without any Spring
Profile, we use the value default as the default
profile. The default return format is in JSON,
and the important points of this are the
property sources. Notice that the bottom
property source is the application.properties.
That's the global properties that applies to
every application. And then the property
source above that, which overrides any of the
global property sources, is the config-clien-
app.properties.

{"name":"config-client-app","profiles":
["prod"],"label":null,"version":"5bbcc634f016351eecb0aaf67650c378e9
425200","state":null,"propertySources":
[{"name":"https://github.com/ajaycucek/config-
repository.git/config-client-app-prod.properties","source":
{"some.property":"profile specific
value","some.other.property":"profile specific value"}},
{"name":"https://github.com/ajaycucek/config-repository.git/config-
client-app.properties","source":{"some.property":"app specific
overridden value"}},{"name":"https://github.com/ajaycucek/config-
repository.git/application.properties","source":
{"some.property":"global","some.other.property":"global"}}]}

Formatting above response :

```
{
  "name":"config-client-app",
  "profiles":[
    "prod"
  ],
  "label":null,

 "version":"5bbcc634f016351eecb0aaf67650c3
78e9425200",
  "state":null,
  "propertySources":[
    {

 "name":"https://github.com/ajaycucek/config
-repository.git/config-client-app-
prod.properties",
      "source":{
        "some.property":"profile specific
value",
        "some.other.property":"profile
specific value"
    }
  },
  {
```

```
    "name":"https://github.com/ajaycucek/config
-repository.git/config-client-app.properties",
      "source":{
        "some.property":"app specific
overridden value"
      }
    },
    {

  "name":"https://github.com/ajaycucek/config
-repository.git/application.properties",
      "source":{
        "some.property":"global",
        "some.other.property":"global"
      }
    }
  ]
}
```

If we modify the URL and replace default
with prod, we'll see that it brings in the config-
client-app-prod.properties file, which
overrides all of the property sources below it.
Don't forget that we also have a couple other
endpoints, like an endpoint to request the
.properties file or the .yml file.

```
some.other.property: global
some.property: app specific overridden value
```

So if we go up here, we take out /prod and we
replace it with .properties, we'll see that it
returns back a properties file. And you'll see
that it's actually applied all of the property
sources in the order which take precedence.
So you see that some.other.property is still
global, but some.property was overridden by
the app specific overridden value.

```
some:
  other:
    property: global
  property: app specific overridden value
```

And you can do the same thing with YAML. It will actually convert the source.properties files into YAML format for you. So instead of .properties, we'll replace this with .yml, and we hit Return, and you can see that it output the same configuration in YAML format.

Using the Spring Cloud Config Client

Now that we've seen how the Spring Cloud Config Server works and how to get one set up, let's look at the other end of the equation, the Client. At its core, the Config Client is responsible for bootstrapping and fetching application configuration. So what do I mean when I say that the Config Client is responsible for bootstrapping application configuration? Well, when a Spring application starts up, it needs to resolve its property sources. And it needs to do that very early on in the startup process. Some of the reasons for that are things like your property placeholders. When you resolve those, it needs to actually have the values to resolve the placeholders. And since the configuration lives on the Configuration Server, that means that the Config Client needs to fetch the application configuration before the Spring application context has even technically started. If it waited until the application was fully started, it would be too late in the process. There are two different ways that you can get the Config Client to bootstrap your application properties, and they both use a special file called the bootstrap.properties or the bootstrap.yml. The first way is Config First, and you do that by configuring a bootstrap.yml or a bootstrap.properties that has the application name, as well as the URL to the Configuration Server. The second way is Discovery First, and that's using service discovery. So you would configure your bootstrap.properties or bootstrap.yml to have the application name and then the location of the Service Discovery Server. And it would use that to then find the Config Server so that it could fetch your configuration. Setting up an application to use the Spring Cloud Config Client is even easier than setting up the Spring Cloud Config Server.

pom.xml :

```
<dependencyManagement>
  <dependencies>
    <dependency>
      <groupId>org.springframework.cloud</groupId>
      <artifactId>spring-cloud-dependencies</artifactId>
      <version>Camden.SR2</version>
      <type>pom</type>
      <scope>import</scope>
    </dependency>
  </dependencies>
</dependencyManagement>
```

In your pom.xml, you import the spring-cloud-dependencies within the dependencyManagement section.

```
<dependency>
```

```
<groupId>org.springframework.cloud
</groupId>
      <artifactId>spring-cloud-config-
client</artifactId>
</dependency
```

Then within the dependency section, still within your pom.xml, define a new dependency on spring-cloud-config-client. Then we need to configure how the Config Client will bootstrap the configuration. If you're using Config First, you define a bootstrap.properties or a bootstrap.yml. bootstrap.properties :

```
spring.application.name=<your_app_name>
spring.cloud.config.uri–http://localhost:8888/
```

OR

```
bootstrap.yml :
spring:application:name: <your_app_name>
cloud:config:uri: http://localhost:8888/
```

And you define the spring.application.name property, and this is the name of your application. It will use this when it calls the Spring Cloud Config Server's REST services to find the appropriate configuration. And then the next property is the spring.cloud.config.uri property, and you would set that to the location of your Config Server. And in this example I've just used localhost here. If you're using a Discovery First configuration to bootstrap the Config Client, the configuration is similar to the one we just looked at, but it's slightly different. bootstrap.properties :

```
spring.application.name=<your_app_name>
spring.cloud.config.discovery.enabled=true
```

OR

```
bootstrap.yml :
spring:application:name: <your_app_name>
cloud:discovery:enabled: true
```

You of course have your bootstrap.properties or your bootstrap.yml, and note that I've only included the differences between the Config First configuration. And that's to define the spring.cloud.config.discovery.enabled property and setting that to true. And you would define that instead of the location of the Config Server. You would also need to make sure that you added your Eureka Client dependencies and your pom.xml. And configure the service URL to the Service Discover Server, and then add the @EnableDiscoveryClient annotation.

Demo: Retrieving Configuration with the Config Client

In this demo, we'll see how to use the Spring Cloud Config Client to retrieve configuration at startup from the Configuration Server. To get started, head on over to start.spring.io. For the Group ID, use io.ajay.kumar. For the Artifact name, use config-client-app. For the dependencies, we're going to want the Config Client, of course, we're going to want Eureka Discovery so that we can use service discovery to find the Configuration Server, and we'll want the Spring Actuator. Once you've got everything selected, click the Generate Project button. That will generate a zip file. Click on that, unzip it, and head over to your IDE.

- ∨ ⊡ config-client-app [boot]
  - ∨ ⊞ src/main/java
    - ∨ ⊞ io.ajay.kumar.configclientapp
      - › ⒥ ConfigClientAppApplication.java
  - ∨ ⊞ src/main/resources
    - ⌀ application.properties
  - ∨ ⊞ src/test/java
    - ∨ ⊞ io.ajay.kumar.configclientapp
      - › ⒥ ConfigClientAppApplicationTests.java
  - › ⬛ JRE System Library [JavaSE-1.8]
  - › ⬛ Maven Dependencies
  - › ⌂ src
  - ⌂ target
  - ⬚ mvnw
  - ⬚ mvnw.cmd
  - Ⓜ pom.xml

Within IntelliJ or Eclipse, right-click on the empty area of the Package Explorer, go to Import, search for Existing Maven Projects, choose that, click Next, browse to the location of your downloaded zip file, mine's in Downloads config-client-app, hit Open, and click Finish.

We're going to be using service discovery to locate the Config Server from the Config Client app. So if you haven't already completed the Service Discovery module, you'll need the Discovery Server and import it into your IDE. It's pretty simple. Next we need to make a couple of modifications to the Config Server so that it will register itself with the Discovery Server.

package io.ajay.kumar.configserver;
import
org.springframework.boot.SpringApplication;
import
org.springframework.boot.autoconfigure.Spri
ngBootApplication;

```
import
org.springframework.cloud.client.discovery.E
nableDiscoveryClient;
import
org.springframework.cloud.config.server.Ena
bleConfigServer;
@SpringBootApplication
@EnableConfigServer
@EnableDiscoveryClient
public class ConfigServerApplication {
    public static void main(String[] args) {
        SpringApplication.run(ConfigServer
Application.class, args);
    }
}
```

Expand the config-server and go to the main application class. Underneath the @EnableConfigServer add an @EnableDiscoveryClient annotation. Save that, and then open up the application.properties in the src/main/resources.

application.properties :
server.port=8888
spring.cloud.config.server.git.uri=https://githu
b.com/ajaycucek/config-repository.git
spring.application.name=configserver
eureka.client.server-
url.defaultZone=https://localhost:8761/eureka

We'll add two different properties. The first one is the spring.application.name, and we're going to set that equal to configserver. No spaces. And then we also want to set the location of the Discovery Server so it knows where to register itself. So we do eureka.client.server-url.defaultZone, and then we set that to localhost:8761/eureka. Next, expand the config-client-app project, and open up the main application class. Remember that there's no special annotation that we need to add for the Config Client to get its configuration. As long as the libraries are on the class path and the setup is correct, it should be able to find the configuration from the Configuration Server.

```
package io.ajay.kumar.configclientapp;
import
org.springframework.boot.SpringApplication;
import
org.springframework.boot.autoconfigure.Spri
ngBootApplication;
import
org.springframework.cloud.client.discovery.E
nableDiscoveryClient;
@SpringBootApplication
@EnableDiscoveryClient
public class ConfigClientAppApplication {
    public static void main(String[] args) {
        SpringApplication.run(ConfigClient
AppApplication.class, args);
    }
}
```

However, we do want to participate in service discovery, so let's add the @EnableDiscoveryClient annotation. Go ahead and save that. Next let's create a new class. So New, Class, and we're going to call this class the ConfigClientAppConfiguration class. Go ahead and click Finish.

```
package io.ajay.kumar.configclientapp;
import
org.springframework.boot.context.properties.
ConfigurationProperties;
Import
org.springframework.stereotype.Component;
@Component
@ConfigurationProperties(prefix="some")
public class ConfigClientAppConfiguration {
```

81

```
    private String property;
    public String getProperty() {
        return property;
    }
    public void setProperty(String property)
{
        this.property = property;
    }
}
```

Let's go ahead and annotate this with @Component and also @ConfigurationProperties. And we're going to give this a prefix equal to some. This ConfigurationProperties is going to represent our property that's named some.property. We'll have an instance variable that is a string, so private String. And the name of it is called property, again, to represent some.property. And make sure that you don't forget the getters and setters. You can do that by going to Source, Generate Getters and Setters, choose the property, click OK, and save that file. Head back to the main application class, and let's autowire our configuration properties class.

```
package io.ajay.kumar.configclientapp;
import
org.springframework.beans.factory.annotatio
n.Autowired;
import
org.springframework.beans.factory.annotatio
n.Value;
import
org.springframework.boot.SpringApplication;
import
org.springframework.boot.autoconfigure.Spri
ngBootApplication;
```

```java
import
org.springframework.cloud.client.discovery.E
nableDiscoveryClient;
import
org.springframework.web.bind.annotation.Re
questMapping;
import
org.springframework.web.bind.annotation.Re
stController;
@SpringBootApplication
@EnableDiscoveryClient
@RestController
public class ConfigClientAppApplication {
    @Autowired
    private ConfigClientAppConfiguration
properties;
    @Value("${some.other.property}")
    private String someOtherProperty;

    public static void main(String[] args) {
        SpringApplication.run(ConfigClient
AppApplication.class, args);
    }

    @RequestMapping
    public String printConfig() {
        StringBuilder sb = new
StringBuilder();
        sb.append(properties.getProperty());
        sb.append(" || ");
        sb.append(someOtherProperty);

        return sb.toString();
    }
}
```
So go in here, we're going to do private
ConfigClientAppConfiguration, and we'll call
this properties. And we'll @Autowired it. You
could also use @Inject here. We'll add

another instance variable, private String someOtherProperty, and we're going to give this an @Value annotation. And we're going to use the placeholder format to inject the someOtherProperty value, so $ curly some.other.property and end curly. Now we're going to add an @RestController annotation to the main application class. So come up here underneath the @EnableDiscoveryClient, and you're going to do @RestController. Go ahead and save that. And note that you normally wouldn't put a REST controller on your main application class; however, since we're just demoing here and we're trying to solidify some concepts, it's okay for now. We also need to add the handler method, so come down here under main, do public String printConfig. And then we're going to annotate this with @RequestMapping. In the body of the method, we're going to construct a string that has the values of each of the configuration properties that were retrieved from the Configuration Server. So we're going to need a string builder, so StringBuilder sb = new StringBuilder. And then we're going to say sb.append. And then we're going to get the first value, which is properties.getProperty. And then we're going to separate it with a double pipe, so sb.append, space, ||, space, and then sb.append the someOtherProperty value. And last, we want to return sb.toString. Next, let's go ahead and close both of these files. And within the src/main/resources, create a new file called bootstrap.properties. bootstrap.properties :
spring.application.name=config-client-app
spring.cloud.config.discovery.enabled=true
eureka.client.server-url.defaultZone=http://localhost:8761/eureka

Within the bootstrap.properties, set the spring.application.name property to the value config-client-app. Then we're going to set another property which tells the Config Client to find the Config Server via service discovery, so spring.cloud.config.discovery.enabled=true. We have one last property to set, and that's the location of the Discovery Server. We've already configured that in the Config Server, so if you want, you can open up the application.properties from the config-server, copy the eureka.client.server URL, and paste that into your bootstrap.properties. We can close all of the configuration files and minimize all of the projects. We're now ready to start running the applications. We'll start by starting the Discovery Server. Navigate to the main application class of the Discovery Server, right-click on it, Run As Spring Boot App. Once the Discovery Server's started, we'll start the Configuration Server next. Go to the main application class of the Config Server, right-click on it, Run As Spring Boot App. And last, we'll start the Config Client. So go to the main application of the Config Client, right-click on it, and Run As Spring Boot App. Now you see that the config-client-app shutting down unexpectedly after registering with Eureka server.
In console you will see :
Shutting down DiscoveryClient ...
config-client-app - registration status: 204
Unregistering ...
config-client-app - deregister status: 200
Completed shut down of DiscoveryClient
Now to fix it add below dependency in pom.xml:

```
<dependency>
<groupId>org.springframework.boot</groupI
d>            <artifactId>spring-boot-starter-
web</artifactId>
</dependency>
```
Now start again.

If you expand the console and scroll up, you'll see that it fetched the configuration from the Configuration Server. So let's open up a browser and visit the Config Client app and see that it resolved those configuration values.

app specific overridden value || global

In your browser, visit localhost:8080, and you'll see that it's resolved the configuration values. The first one, the app specific overridden value is the value from the some.property property. And remember we set that to this app specific overridden value in the Config Client configuration. And then the next property, separated by the ||, the global, is coming from the global properties, the application.properties.

Updating Configuration at Runtime

Updating configuration at runtime is easily one of the best features of Spring Cloud. With it, you can do things like refresh your @ConfigurationProperties at runtime. You can also use it to update the logging levels on any piece of code. And the changes happen almost instantaneously. And the best part is that you can do all of this without ever restarting your application. So how do you do it? Well, the first step is updating your configuration. And you do that by cloning the configuration repository that your Config Server is looking at, make your changes, and then git add, git commit, and git push your changes up to the configuration repository. From there, there are several different ways that the application gets the new configuration, both manually and automatically.

- /refresh with spring-boot-actuator
- /bus/refresh with spring-cloud-bus
- VCS + /monitor with spring-cloud-config-monitor & spring-cloud-bus

The first way is manually, and that's by calling the refresh endpoint that's included in the Spring Actuator project. And just to be clear, you would need to do that for every individual service that needs its configuration updated. The second way is a combination of both manual and automatic. And you can imagine that if you had a lot of servers, calling the refresh endpoint on each of them manually could be a pretty painful process. Instead, if each of the applications were to subscribe to an event, and you were to call the bus/refresh endpoint, Spring Cloud Bus would send out a message to all of the subscribers indicating to them that they need to refresh their configuration. Now note that there isn't any sort of intelligence in whether or not the configuration changed. Every subscriber goes and gets its new configuration regardless. The third way is just like the second except for it adds a level of intelligence. And the way it does that is you hook it up into your virgin control system, like Git, and any time you make a commit, the changeset of the commit is posted to a monitor endpoint, and then that monitor endpoint can determine which services need to have their configuration updated. So let's visualize this. Imagine that you made a commit to some configuration, and you pushed that up to the configuration repository. And the repository knows what changed, and it sent that changeset to the monitor endpoint, and then it decided that it only needed to notify two of the three applications to update their configuration. Regardless of which method you chose to notify your applications about configuration updates, there's one last step. And that is to celebrate. You can brag to your colleagues about making configuration changes on the fly without ever restarting your application. And you can do it all at once or even all automatically. And last, since you used Git, you have a full audit log of all of the changes that you've made to your configuration.

Utilizing the @RefreshScope Annotation

We've already talked about how @ConfigurationProperties and logging levels will be updated when configuration is refreshed, but unfortunately that doesn't cover all of the use cases. Anything that gets its value only at initialization time, like an @Bean or an @Value, will not be automatically refreshed like the others. To understand this a little bit better, it helps to see an example.

```
@Configuration
public class SomeConfiguration{
    @Bean
    public FooService
    fooService(FooProperties properties){
    return new
    FooService(properties.getConfigValue(
    ));
    }
}
```

Example: @Bean Will Not See New Config Value After a Refresh

- **Configuration updates are made**
    - **Note that FooProperties is a @ConfigurationProperties class**
- **POST to /refresh**
- **Result: FooService will still contain the OLD configuration value**
    - **Only gets configuration during initialization**

Suppose you have an @Configuration class, and it declares a new bean called FooService. And to construct FooService, you need to give it a configuration value from FooProperties, which is an argument to the bean method. And FooProperties is an @Configuration class. Then you make some configuration changes to the properties that are bound to FooProperties, and you issue a POST request to the refresh endpoint. If you were to look at FooService at this point, even though you called refresh, it would actually still have the old configuration value. And that's because it only gets its configuration during initialization. Here's another example.

```
@Configuration
public class SomeConfiguration{
    @Value("${some.config.value}")
    String configValue;
```

```
    @Bean
    public FooService fooService(){
            return new
    FooService(configValue);
    }
}
```

Example: @Value Will Not See New Config Value After a Refresh

- Configuration updates are made
- POST to /refresh
- Result: FooServicewill still contain the OLDconfiguration value
  - Only gets configuration during initialization

Again, we have an @Configuration class, and this time we have an @Value annotation that has some configuration that needs to be injected. And we'll use that configuration as a constructor argument to construct the FooService bean. So we go through the same process; we update some configuration, we POST to the refresh endpoint, and again we realize that our configuration value is still the old value. It did not get updated. By now you have to be wondering how do I refresh an @Bean or an @Value that only gets its configuration during initialization? And the answer to that is with the @RefreshScope annotation. Let's go back to our first example and see how and where we utilize the @RefreshScope annotation.

```
@Configuration
public class SomeConfiguration{
    @Bean @RefreshScope
    public FooService
    fooService(FooProperties properties){
    return new
    FooService(properties.getConfigValue(
    ));
```

```
        }
}
```
Example: Utilizing @RefreshScope
- Add the @RefreshScope annotation to the @Bean
- POST to /refresh
- Result: FooService will now contain the NEW configuration value!
  - @RefreshScopetells Spring to please reinitialize this @Bean

In your @Configuration class, all you need to do is add the @RefreshScope annotation to your @Bean. And once you POST to the refresh endpoint, FooService will now see the latest configuration value. RefreshScope works just like it sounds. It's a hint to Spring that this @Bean or this @Value should be included in the scope of the refresh.

Demo: Refresh Configuration Without Restarting Your App

In this demo, we'll learn how to refresh our configuration at runtime, as well as how to use the @RefreshScope annotation. Before we get started with the demo, make sure that you have a tool called Postman installed. You can get it by going to www.getpostman.com. And we'll use this tool to call the REST endpoints. It's a nice little REST client. The first thing we'll do is start all of our applications, so go ahead and start the Discovery Server, the Config Server, and the Config Client app.. Now remember that you need to start them in the correct order. So the Discovery Server first, then the Config Server, then the Config

Client app. So if you have any problems with starting them, make sure that you start them in that order. Open up a browser and visit localhost:8080.

← → C ⓘ localhost:8080

app specific overridden value || global

And you'll see the configuration values that got resolved from the Configuration Server. Now, we want to update each of these values, so we're going to update the first one, the app specific overridden value, and the global one. So, head back to the IDE. Back in the IDE, expand the config-repository project, and open up the config-client-app.properties file. config-client-app.properties :
# Put application-specific config here (application name: client-config-app)
some.property=coffee
some.other.property=is good
And we're going to change this from the app specific overridden value to coffee. And then we're also going to set the other one. We're going to override the some.other.property, and we're going to say is good. Go ahead and save those. Close that file. And then we're going to commit those changes, so right-click on the scf-config-repository, go to Team, go to Commit, type in a commit message, Updating configuration, and click the Commit and Push. And it'll pop up a new dialog showing you that it pushed those changes. Just go ahead and click OK. And you can exit out of that Git Staging view. So now we've updated the configuration, and we've pushed it to the configuration repository. And if you go back to your browser and you refresh the page, the value should still be the old values.

We haven't explicitly asked the application to refresh its configuration. In order to do that, start up the Postman application, and on the New Tab where it says GET, click that drop-down and choose POST. Then in the request URL type http://localhost:8080/refresh. Once you've got that typed in, hit Send, and the server will respond back with all of the properties that changed. So there's an internal property that it has called the config.client.verion, as well as the two other properties that we changed, the some.other.property and the some.property. Head back to your browser and refresh the page.

coffee || global

And ooh, that's interesting. The first value refreshed for us, we got the coffee value that we set in, but the second value is still pointing to the global configuration value. And the reason for that is that the second value is retrieved using the @Value annotation, and @Value annotations are not automatically refreshed when you call the refresh endpoint. So we can fix that with the @RefreshScope annotation. Back within the IDE, stop the Config Client app. Then in the main application class, let's find the someOtherProperty. So we have here the @Value annotation that gets the some.other.property value. So to fix our problem of the @Value annotation not

93

updating, let's add the @RefreshScope to the main application class.

```java
package io.ajay.kumar.configclientapp;
import org.springframework.beans.factory.annotation.Autowired;
import org.springframework.beans.factory.annotation.Value;
import org.springframework.boot.SpringApplication;
import org.springframework.boot.autoconfigure.SpringBootApplication;
import org.springframework.cloud.client.discovery.EnableDiscoveryClient;
import org.springframework.cloud.context.config.annotation.RefreshScope;
import org.springframework.web.bind.annotation.RequestMapping;
import org.springframework.web.bind.annotation.RestController;
@SpringBootApplication
@EnableDiscoveryClient
@RestController
@RefreshScope
public class ConfigClientAppApplication {
    @Autowired
    private ConfigClientAppConfiguration properties;
    @Value("${some.other.property}")
    private String someOtherProperty;

    public static void main(String[] args) {
```

```
        SpringApplication.run(ConfigClient
AppApplication.class, args);
    }


    @RequestMapping
    public String printConfig() {
        StringBuilder sb = new
StringBuilder();
        sb.append(properties.getProperty());
        sb.append(" || ");
        sb.append(someOtherProperty);
        return sb.toString();
    }
}
```

So you type @RefreshScope. Go ahead and save that and restart the application. Now since we restarted the application, the application's going to fetch the latest configuration values when it starts up. So we won't actually be demonstrating the use of @RefreshScope because it's going to get the latest value regardless. And so what we need to do is we need to update the value again. So go ahead and open up the config-client-app, and change this some.other.property to is really good.

config-client-app.properties :

# Put application-specific config here (application name: client-config-app)
some.property=coffee
some.other.property=is really good

Save that, close that file out, and again commit that up to the Git repository. So Team, Commit, updating configuration again, and click the Commit and Push button. You can exit the Git Staging view. And head back to your browser and refresh the page.

coffee ‖ is good

As you can see, it says coffee is good. And is good is the value that it retrieved on start up. But once we refresh this with the refresh scope now added, it will fetch the latest value for that @Value annotation. So go ahead and open up Postman, and on the New Tab where it says GET, click that drop-down and choose POST. Then in the request URL type http://localhost:8080/refresh. Once you've got that typed in, hit Send, and you can see it changed the some.other.property. Head back to the browser, and refresh that page.

coffee ‖ is really good

And you can see that it changed our property this time from is good to is really good.

Encrypting and Decrypting Sensitive Configuration

Spring Cloud Config Server also provides additional useful functionality for encrypting and decrypting your configuration. It has support for several different features.
Supported features :

- Encrypted configuration at rest and/or in-flight
- An /encrypt endpoint to encrypt configuration
- A /decrypt endpoint to decrypt configuration

- **Encrypting and decrypting with symmetric or asymmetric keys**

It supports encrypted configuration at rest or in-flight. And at rest, that simply just means that your configuration is encrypted when it's stored on disc. And in-flight means that it's encrypted as it travels between the Config Server and the Config Client. It has utility endpoints for encrypting and decrypting your configuration. And one really important thing to point out is that by default neither of these endpoints are secured unless you configure security for your Configuration Server. And we've already talked about how to secure your Config Server. And remember that any of the methods that are supported by Spring Security will also work for securing your Config Server. And last, it has support for encrypting and decrypting using either symmetric or asymmetric keys. So you can choose whatever works best for your situation. Before we get into the details on encrypting and decrypting configuration, I thought it would be useful to see how encrypted configuration looks.

application.properties :
my.datasource.username=foobar
my.datasource.password={cipher}ASFIOWR ODSKSDFIR32KJL
application.yml :
my:datasource:username: foobar
password:
'{cipher}ASFIOWRODSKSDFIR32KJL'

I've included both an application.properties and an application.yml. And they both have the same encrypted database password. Notice that before the random letters and numbers there's a special value of cipher, and it's surrounded by curly braces. This is what denotes that the real value is an encrypted value. And notice that there's one minor difference in the application.yml versus the properties. The YAML file requires us to surround the value in single quotes, whereas the properties file does not. Now that you've seen what encrypted configuration looks like, you're probably wondering at what point is the configuration decrypted? And there are two different options. The first option is upon request, and that's at the Configuration Server. So you make a request for configuration for a specific application, and the Config Server decrypts the values in the configuration before sending it back. You'd only want to use this if the connection between your Config Server and your Config Client is secure. If it's not, you can utilize the second option that decrypts the value's client side. And this is exactly opposite of the first option. Instead of decrypting the values before sending them back, the Config Server sends them in encrypted format, and the client is responsible for decrypting them. Note that the default way is the first option, upon request. And if you want the client to decrypt the configuration, you have to set a property on the Config Server, spring.cloud.config.server.encrypt.enabled, that's a big one, =false. And that will tell the Config Server not to decrypt the values before sending them back to the client.

Using the Encryption and Decryption Support

Before we get into the details about configuring our Configuration Server for encryption and decryption support, note that it assumes we have the Java Cryptography Extension installed, or commonly referred to as JCE.

Step One: Choose Your Key Type

- Symmetric Key
- Asymmetric Key

  - Public Key
  - Private Key

The first step to encrypting your configuration is to choose the key type, and that could be either symmetric or asymmetric. And typically symmetric keys are easier to use, but less secure than asymmetric keys. And you can choose whatever works best for your situation.

Step Two (Symmetric): Configure the Config Server

application.properties :
encrypt.key=<your_super_secret_key>
application.yml :
encrypt:key: <your_super_secret_key>

Step two, if you're using a symmetric key, is to configure the encryption key. And you can do that in the application.properties or the application.yml. And the property that is set is encrypt.key. And you would set that to the secret value you'll use to encrypt your configuration.

Step Two (Asymmetric): Configure the Config Server Option 1

application.properties :

encrypt.key=<pem_encoded_key_as_text>

application.yml :

encrypt:key: <pem_encoded_key_as_text>

Step two, if you're using asymmetric keys, can be done in two different ways. The first way is to set the value of the encrypt.key property in the application.properties or the application.yml as a pem_encoded_key_as_text. And the PEM encoded key would contain both the public and the private key.

Step Two (Asymmetric): Configure the Config Server Option 2

application.properties :

encrypt.keyStore.location=<path_to_keystore >

encrypt.keyStore.password=<keystore_passwo rd>

encrypt.keyStore.alias=<key_name_in_keysto re>

application.yml :

encrypt:keyStore:location:

<path_to_keystore>

password: <key_name_in_keystore>

alias: <key_name_in_keystore>

The second way, if you're using asymmetric keys, is to use the Java KeyStore. Once you've created or imported your public and private key into an existing or new keystore, you simply configure the location of the keystore, the password to the keystore, and the name of the alias that you chose when creating or importing the key into the keystore. And you can do that in the application.properties, of course, or in the application.yml.

Encrypt and Decrypt REST Endpoints

Once you have your Config Server all set up for cryptography, you can utilize some of the utility REST endpoints to encrypt and decrypt values that you will put or take out of your configuration. Both of the endpoints are really, really easy to use.
Utility REST Endpoints: Encrypt Values

- Endpoint

  - POST /encrypt

- Example

  - Request: /encrypt
  - Data: <value_to_encrypt>

The first one is the encrypt endpoint, and you'd use this to generate the encrypted values that you'll use in your configuration. And it's really simple to use, like I said. All you do is send a POST request to the /encrypt endpoint, and you pass the value that you want to encrypt as the body of the request. The Config Server will use its configured key, either the symmetric or the asymmetric key, to encrypt that value. And again, I can't stress this enough, make sure that this endpoint is secure using Spring Security or any other means to

ensure that this endpoint is only accessed by authorized users.
Utility REST Endpoints: Decrypt Values

- **Endpoint**

    - **POST /decrypt**

- **Example**

    - **Request: /decrypt**
    - **Data: <value_to_decrypt>**

The decrypt endpoint is literally almost identical to the encrypt endpoint with the exception of the name and the inputs. And you'd mainly use this for debugging purposes. So to decrypt a value, you would POST to /decrypt, and you would send the encrypted value as the body of the request, and it would return to you the unencrypted value.

Summary

- **The explosion of configuration in the cloud and the need for a config server**
- **Using the Spring Cloud Config Server & Client**
- **Updating configuration at runtime without restarting**
- **Encrypting and decrypting configuration**

We've reached the end of this module, so let's take a moment to review what we've learned. We've covered a lot of topics. We first talked about the need for a Configuration Server in a cloud environment to manage the explosion of configuration that comes with managing a distributed system. Then, we saw how to configure the Spring Cloud Config Server to serve our configuration files and how to use the Spring Cloud Config Client along with the bootstrap.properties or the bootstrap.yml to retrieve the configuration during application initialization. After that, we saw how we could brag to our colleagues about updating our configuration at runtime without ever needing to restart our application server. We also saw what gets automatically refreshed and what requires an @RefreshScope annotation. And last, we finished out the module with a section on how to utilize the encryption and decryption support within Spring Cloud Config.

Module 5: Mapping Services Using Intelligent Routing

What Is Intelligent Routing?

In this module we'll learn how to map our services in the cloud using Intelligent Routing.

- Routing in cloud native apps
- Netflix Zuul

  - Proxy server
  - Setting up routes
  - Setting up filters

We'll begin by talking about what Intelligent Routing is and what problem it solves for us. Then we'll introduce Netflix Zuul as part of the Spring Cloud Netflix project. And we'll see how to set up a proxy server, how to configure different routes, and how to set up filtering. Remember that in order to be as dynamic and as scalable as possible, a cloud-native system is made up of individually deployable services, which together, as a whole, form an overall system. With that comes some challenges though.

Challenges with Individual Services

- Different ports
- Different addresses
- Different APIs & paths

Each of the individual services may be running on a different port, a different address, or a combination of both. And they'll also likely have different paths and different APIs to interact with. And as a user or a client of those services, such as a mobile app or a web app, interacting with each of the individual services, which could easily be in the double or triple digits, would be a nightmare. Instead, we can use Intelligent Routing to make our application appear as if it were a single system. Similar to how a completed puzzle appears as if it were a whole, but it's made up of several different individual pieces.

Intelligent Routing via a Gateway Service

Routing is typically implemented via something called a gateway service, or an API Gateway. And an API Gateway, or a gateway service, is defined as the single point of entry for all clients. So in many ways the gateway service is a lot like the front door to our system. And each of the individual services is then located behind this door, and all the requests must enter through it.

A Gateway Service Provides

- **Dynamic Routing & Delivery**
- **Security & Filtering**
- **Auditing & Logging**
- **Request Enhancement**
- **Load Balancing**
- **Different APIs for different clients**

A gateway service not only provides dynamic routing and delivery, which means at runtime it can decide where it should route a request and if it should even route a request at all, but it also provides an array of other functionalities. One of those pieces of functionality is security. It provides the ability to authenticate all of the incoming requests, as well as filter out any sort of illegitimate or bad request. And it's actually a really good candidate for providing auditing and logging of requests since all of the requests must enter through the gateway. It also provides something called request enhancement, which is just a fancy way of saying that it can add additional information to the request, or enrich the request, if you will. A concrete example of this is the way Netflix uses their gateway. They use their gateway service to do a geolocation lookup for all incoming requests, and they add that additional information as an additional request header so that it's available for all downstream services. The gateway service can also act as a load balancer for the individual services that are behind it. Another interesting feature of the gateway service is the ability to provide different APIs for different clients. APIs are not a one-size-fits-all kind of thing, and different clients, such as web clients or mobile clients, have different needs in the way they call your APIs. So, for instance, it may be okay for a web client to interact with several endpoints to accomplish some piece of functionality, but the same may not be true for a mobile client, which may be better served with just a single endpoint.

Using Netflix Zuul with Spring Cloud

Intelligent Routing is implemented using a combination of Spring Cloud and a project from Netflix. The project is called Netflix Zuul, and it's pronounced zool, which rhymes with the word tool. The project page for the Netflix Zuul project defines it as a gateway service that provides dynamic routing, monitoring, resiliency, security, and more.

And the name Zuul is actually a pretty good name as Zuul refers to a fictional, monster-like character in the movie Ghostbusters that's the gatekeeper just like a gateway service is the gatekeeper. We'll talk about how you go about adding Spring Cloud and Netflix Zuul to a project, and then we'll follow up with a live demo. Just like all of the other Spring Cloud projects, adding Spring Cloud and Netflix Zuul to your project is really, really easy.

Using Spring Cloud & Netflix Zuul
pom.xml :

```
<dependencyManagement>
  <dependencies>
    <dependency>

<groupId>org.springframework.cloud</groupId>
      <artifactId>spring-cloud-
dependencies</artifactId>
      <version>Camden.SR2</version>
      <type>pom</type>
      <scope>import</scope>
    </dependency>
  </dependencies>
</dependencyManagement>
```

In the dependencyManagement section of the pom.xml, define a new dependency with a scope of import on spring-cloud-dependencies.

```
<dependency>

<groupId>org.springframework.cloud</groupId>
  <artifactId>spring-cloud-starter-
zuul</artifactId>
</dependency>
```

And still within the pom.xml, define a new dependency in the dependency section on spring-cloud-starter-zuul.

```
@SpringBootApplication
@EnableZuulProxy
public class Application{
   public static void main(String[] args){
      SpringApplication.run(Application.class,
args);
   }
}
```

Then, in your main Application class, add the @EnableZuulProxy annotation, and this is the annotation that turns your application into the gateway service. From a configuration standpoint, you have two different options. You can configure your gateway service to use service discovery or you can configure it without service discovery.

Using Spring Cloud & Netflix Zuul with Service Discovery

```
application.properties :
spring.application.name=gateway-service
eureka.client.defaultZone=http://localhost:876
1/eureka
```

OR

```
application.yml :
spring:application:name: gateway-service
eureka:client:defaultZone:
http://localhost:8761/eureka
```

If you're using service discovery, define the usual parameters for the name of the application and the location of the Service Discovery Server.

Using Spring Cloud & Netflix Zuul Without Service Discovery

```
application.properties :
spring.application.name=gateway-service
ribbon.eureka.enabled=false
```

OR
application.yml :
spring:application:name: gateway-service
ribbon:eureka:enabled: false
If you're not using service discovery, you still
define the application name, and you add an
additional parameter,
ribbon.eureka.enabled=false. Remember how
I mentioned that the gateway service can serve
as a load balancer for your services? Well, the
name of the client-side load balancer project
from Netflix is called Ribbon. And we'll get
into more details about what Ribbon is in the
module on client-side load balancing.

Configuring Routes in Netflix Zuul

Once you have everything configured, the next
step is to define how Zuul should route
requests. The default routing behavior when
Zuul is set up using service discovery is to
route requests by service name.
Default Route to Service Resolution with
Service Discovery
Request: /foo   maps to Service:
spring.application.name=foo
Request: /categories/1   maps to Service:
spring.application.name=categories
So for example, if you requested /foo, Zuul
would use service discovery to find the service
with a name of foo and send that request to
that service. Here's another example. If you
were to request /categories/1, Zuul would
locate the service with the name categories,
and it would send the /1 request to that
service. By default, the prefix is stripped from

the request, so the service actually only gets the /1 part of the request. If you wanted it to send the full request, the /categories/1, you could set the property zuul.stripPrefix to false, and the service would get the request /categories/1. Also note that all services are added by default, so you'll want to use the zuul.ignoredServices, and you could set that to a pattern to ignore specific services.

Netflix Zuul with Service Discovery:Precise Routing

application.properties
spring.application.name=gateway-service
zuul.routes.<route_name>.path=/somepath/**
zuul.routes.<route_name>.serviceId=some_service_id
zuul.ignored-services=some_service_id

OR

application.yml
spring:application:name: gateway-service
zuul:routes:<route_name>:path:
/somepath/**
serviceId: some_service_id
ignored-services: some_service_id

In addition to the default configuration, you can also define more precise configuration for specific services. First you define the path with the zuul.routes.route_name.path property where the route name can be anything you want. And the path is defined as a path that's using the Ant-style matchers. Then you define the same property prefix, but end it with service_id instead of path. And the service ID is the service identifier that Zuul will look for when discovering the service via service discovery. You'll also need to set the zuul.ignored-services property so that Zuul doesn't try to automatically add a route for that service ID.

Netflix Zuul Without Service Discovery:Precise Routing

```
application.properties
spring.application.name=gateway-service
zuul.routes.<route_name>.path=/somepath/**
zuul.routes.<route_name>.url=http://some_url_address/
```

OR

```
application.yml
spring:
application:
name: gateway-service
zuul:
routes:
<route_name>:
path: /somepath/**
url: http://some_url_address/
```

The configuration for when you're not using service discovery is actually pretty similar to when you are. You define the path, just like you did in the previous configuration, and then instead of defining a service ID, you simply define the URL to the service.

Demo: Using Netflix Zuul as an Intelligent Router

Head on over to start.spring.io, and we're going to create three different projects here. So for the Group ID do io.ajay.kumar, and for the Artifact, the first one we're going to create, we're going to say gateway-service. For the dependencies, we'll want to add Zuul, and then we'll also want to add Eureka Discovery.

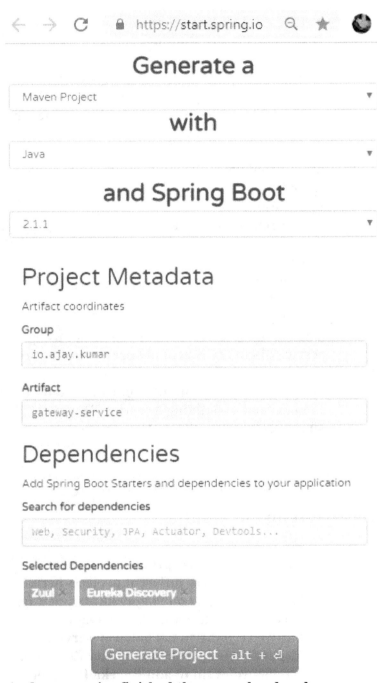

And once you're finished there, go ahead and click Generate Project, and that will create a

zip file for you. And still on the same page, clear the dependencies and change the Artifact to hello-service. And for the dependencies, we'll want to add Web and Eureka Discovery.

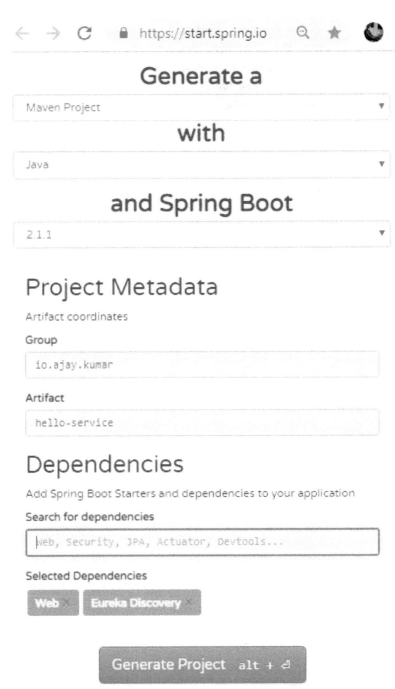

Go ahead and click Generate Project, and that will create a hello-service.zip. And leave

everything the same, but change this from hello to goodbye. So we're going to have a hello and a goodbye-service.

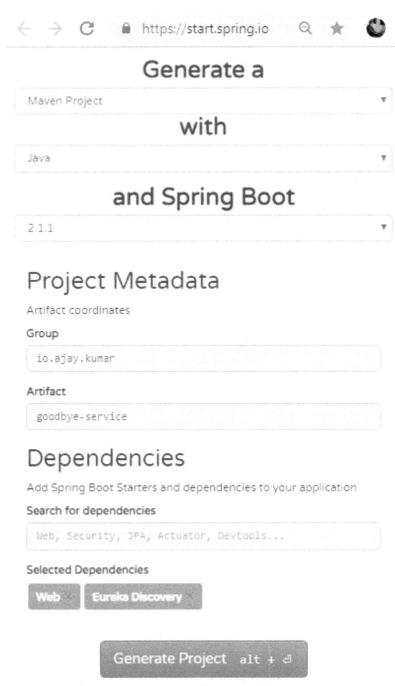

**And click Generate Project. Go ahead and
unzip all of those zip files and head over to**

your IDE. Within your IDE, right-click on the empty space in the Package Explorer, and go to Import, and choose Existing Maven Projects. Navigate to the location of the downloaded zip files, we'll use the gateway-service first, and click Open, and click Finish. And that imports the project into our IDE, and you'll need to do the same for the other two services. I have all of the services imported. We're also going to need the Service Discovery Server, so if you don't already have that imported into your IDE from completing the previous modules, I'll quickly show you how you can import it. Go ahead and right-click on the empty area of the Package Explorer, and go to New, and choose Other. In the textbox, go ahead and start typing maven, and choose the option that says Check out Maven Projects from SCM. Click Next. We'll need to grab the git clone URL from GitHub, so go ahead and fire up a browser and visit github.com/ajaycucek/discovery-server. On the GitHub page, locate the Clone or download button, click it, and highlight the clone URL. Copy that to your clipboard and head back to the IDE. In the textbox under the SCM URL, go ahead and paste that and click Next, and click Finish. We now have everything we need to get started.

- ⌄ 🅼🅂 gateway-service [boot]
  - › 🌿 Spring Elements
  - ⌄ 🕮 src/main/java
    - ⌄ ⊞ io.ajay.kumar.gatewayservice
      - › Ⓙ GatewayServiceApplication.java
  - ⌄ 🕮 src/main/resources
    - 🌿 application.properties
  - ⌄ 🕮 src/test/java
    - ⌄ ⊞ io.ajay.kumar.gatewayservice
      - › Ⓙ GatewayServiceApplicationTests.java
  - › 📚 JRE System Library [JavaSE-1.8]
  - › 📚 Maven Dependencies
  - › 🗁 src
  - › 🗁 target
  - 📄 mvnw
  - 📄 mvnw.cmd
  - Ⓜ pom.xml

Go ahead and expand the gateway-service project, and locate the main application class. In the main application class, we're going to add two annotations. The first one is the @EnableZuulProxy annotation, and the second one is the @EnableDiscoveryClient annotation.

package io.ajay.kumar.gatewayservice;
import org.springframework.boot.SpringApplication;
import org.springframework.boot.autoconfigure.SpringBootApplication;
import org.springframework.cloud.client.discovery.EnableDiscoveryClient;
import org.springframework.cloud.netflix.zuul.EnableZuulProxy;
@SpringBootApplication
@EnableZuulProxy
@EnableDiscoveryClient

```
public class GatewayServiceApplication {
    public static void main(String[] args) {
        SpringApplication.run(GatewayServ
iceApplication.class, args);
    }
}
```
Next, we'll open up the application.properties
and configure the properties for the gateway
service. So go ahead and expand
src/main/resources and open the
application.properties.
application.properties
spring.application.name=gateway-service
eureka.client.service-
url.defaultZone=http://localhost:8761/eureka
The first property we're going to add is the
spring.application.name property, and we're
going to set that to gateway-service. And then
the other property we'll need is the location of
the Service Discovery Server. So we'll say
eureka.client.service-url.defaultZone, and
then we'll set that to localhost:8761/eureka.
Next, you can go ahead and close both of those
files and minimize the gateway-service
project. Next, we're going to open up the
hello-service project, so go ahead and expand
that, and open up the main application class.
package io.ajay.kumar.helloservice;
import
org.springframework.boot.SpringApplication;
import
org.springframework.boot.autoconfigure.Spri
ngBootApplication;
import
org.springframework.cloud.client.discovery.E
nableDiscoveryClient;
import
org.springframework.web.bind.annotation.Re
questMapping;

119
```
```

```java
import
org.springframework.web.bind.annotation.Re
stController;
@SpringBootApplication
@EnableDiscoveryClient
@RestController
public class HelloServiceApplication {
    public static void main(String[] args) {
        SpringApplication.run(HelloService
Application.class, args);
    }
    @RequestMapping
    public String hello() {
        return "Hello!";
    }
}
```

In the main application class, we're going to add the @EnableDiscoveryClient annotation, and we're also going to make this a RestController. Now this is normally a bad idea if you were to do this in a real application, but we're just doing this as a simple example so it's okay for now. So we'll go ahead and add @RestController. Go ahead and save that. And then we'll need a handler method, so public String hello. And this is just going to return Hello!, and we'll annotate this with @RequestMapping. Now we need to configure our hello-service application, so go ahead and open up src/main/resources and open up the application.properties.

application.properties
spring.application.name=hello
server.port=1111
eureka.client.service-
url.defaultZone=http://localhost:8761/eureka

In the application.properties, the first property we'll set is the spring.application.name, and we'll set this to

hello. And we're also going to set the server
port. Since we have multiple applications
running at the same time, we don't want their
ports to conflict. So we'll say server.port, and
we'll set this to 1111. Go ahead and save that.
And then the last property is setting the
location of the Service Discovery Server. And
we can go ahead and just copy that from the
gateway service. So open up the
application.properties from the gateway
service, copy the configuration value that's
setting the location of the Service Discovery
Server, close that, and then paste that into
your application.properties. You're going to
repeat basically the same process for the
goodbye-service except for all of the locations
that it says hello will be goodbye. And instead
of using all 1s for the port, we'll use all 2s. I
completed goodbye-service, so let's take a look
at the main application class.

```
package io.ajay.kumar.goodbyeservice;
import
org.springframework.boot.SpringApplication;
import
org.springframework.boot.autoconfigure.Spri
ngBootApplication;
import
org.springframework.cloud.client.discovery.E
nableDiscoveryClient;
import
org.springframework.web.bind.annotation.Re
questMapping;
import
org.springframework.web.bind.annotation.Re
stController;
@SpringBootApplication
@EnableDiscoveryClient
@RestController
public class GoodbyeServiceApplication {
```

```
    public static void main(String[] args) {
        SpringApplication.run(GoodbyeServ
iceApplication.class, args);
    }
    @RequestMapping
    public String goodbye() {
        return "Goodbye!";
    }
}
```

We have the @EnableDiscoveryClient
annotation and the @RestController
annotation, and then we have one handler
method, which is goodbye, and it's annotated
with the @RequestMapping.
application.properties
spring.application.name=goodbye
server.port=2222
eureka.client.service-
url.defaultZone=http://localhost:8761/eureka
In the application.properties, we have the
spring.application.name set to goodbye and
the server.port set to all 2s. And then the
configuration for the Service Discovery Server
is exactly the same. We're now ready to start
up all of the applications and try them out. So
go ahead and close these files and collapse the
goodbye-service. Open up the discovery-server
service as this is the first application we'll
start. So right-click on that, go to Run As,
choose Spring Boot App. After that, we'll go
ahead and start the gateway service, so right-
click on the main application of the gateway
service, go to Run As, Spring Boot App. And
then we can start the goodbye-service next, so
expand the goodbye-service, and right-click on
the main application class, Run As, Spring
Boot App. And last, we can start the hello-
service application, so right-click on its main
application class, Run As, Spring Boot App.

And just to confirm that you have all of the applications started, you can click little drop-down arrow near display selected console in console window, and you'll see each of the individual services that you have running. Let's open up a browser and try things out. In your browser, visit localhost:8080/hello.

← → C ⓘ localhost:8080/hello

Hello!

And, as you can see, it returned the Hello! string. And just to confirm, we'll also hit the goodbye endpoint.

← → C 🌐 localhost:8080/goodbye

Goodbye!

And, as expected, it returned the Goodbye! string. Now these examples are very simplistic, but a lot is going on in the background. When we visited localhost:8080/goodbye, the gateway service looked up a service with the name goodbye from the Service Discovery Server and then proxied the traffic to that service and then proxied the response back to the browser.

Creating Filters with Netflix Zuul & Spring Cloud

One of the key features in Netflix Zuul is the ability to define filters. Filters allow you to intercept and control the requests and the responses that pass through the gateway. Zuul has support for several different types of filters.
Filter Types

- pre : Before the request
- post : After the request
- route : Direct the request
- error : Handle request errors

The first one is the pre type filter, which is executed before the request is routed. Next comes the route type filter, which allows you to direct the request in any way you want. In fact, earlier when we defined the @EnableZuulProxy annotation on the main application class, we were telling Spring to set up some predefined route filters to proxy our request to back-end services. After route comes the post filters, and, as the name suggests, these filters are executed after the request is routed. And the last one is the error filter type. The error filter type is responsible for handling when any of the previous filter types, the pre, route, or posts, results in an error. To define a Zuul filter, you simply extend and implement the ZuulFilter class.

```
public class MyFilter extends ZuulFilter{
// implement methods
...
}
```

And there are four different methods to implement.

```
@Override public Object run(){
    // Filter logic goes here. Current
implementation ignores return
}
@Override public boolean shouldFilter(){
    // Whether or not the run()method should
execute
}
@Override public String filterType(){
    // The type of filter: pre, route, post, error
```

```
}
@Override public int filterOrder(){
   // The order of execution with respect to
other filters of the same type
}
```

The first is the run method, and this is where the main logic of the filter goes. Note that it returns an object, but the current implementation ignores it so you can just simply return null from this method. The next method is the shouldFilter method, and, as the name suggests, this method allows you to return true or false indicating whether or not the filter should be ran. The third method is the filterType method, and here you can define one of the four predefined values, either pre, route, post, or error. The last method is the filterOrder method, and this allows you to control the execution of your Zuul filters.

```
RequestContext ctx =
RequestContext.getCurrentContext();
HttpServletRequest req = ctx.getRequest();
HttpServletResponse res = ctx.getResponse();
ctx.set("foobar","PRE_FILTER_EXECUTE
D");
String foobar = (String)ctx.get("foobar");
```

Sharing Between Filters: RequestContext holds request, response, state, and data information. Only available for the duration of the request

The RequestContext is an object that's responsible for holding the request, the response, and any state or data information that needs to be shared between all of the filters. So you'd use it to get access to the HttpServletRequest or Response, as well as use it to set or get data for or from other filters. The RequestContext is unique to every request and only lasts the duration of the

request. Once you've defined and implemented your Zuul filter, you need to tell Spring about it.
Creating a Filter: Define an @Bean Which Returns the Filter

```
@Configuration
public class MyConfig{
    @Bean
    public ZuulFilter myFilter(){
        return newMyFilter();
    }
}
```

In your @Configuration class, create a method that returns the Zuul filter and annotate it with @Bean. Spring Cloud Netflix will pick up and add any beans of type ZuulFilter to Zuul.

Demo: Creating and Using a ZuulFilter

In this demo, we'll learn how to implement a Zuul filter to add an additional header to the incoming request so that it's available for downstream services to consume. We'll start from where we left off in the previous demo. And remember that we had four different services. We had the discovery-server that was doing service discovery, we had the gateway-service, which was our edge service, and then we had two application services, the goodbye-service and the hello-service. Since we're building a filter, we'll start off in the gateway-service. So go ahead and expand the gateway-service and create a new package. So go ahead and New, Package, and we'll call this io.ajay.kumar.filters. And within that new package create a new class, so New, Class, and we'll call this AddRequestHeaderFilter. And remember that we have to extend the ZuulFilter class, so the superclass for our class will be ZuulFilter.

```
package io.ajay.kumar.filters;
import com.netflix.zuul.ZuulFilter;
import com.netflix.zuul.context.RequestContext;
public class AddRequestHeaderFilter extends ZuulFilter {
@Override
public boolean shouldFilter() {
 return true;
}
@Override
public Object run() {
 RequestContext ctx =
RequestContext.getCurrentContext();
 ctx.addZuulRequestHeader("x-location",
"USA");
 return null;
}
@Override
public String filterType() {
 return "pre";
}
@Override
public int filterOrder() {
 return 0;
}
}
```

For the first method, the shouldFilter method, let's go ahead and change that from return false to return true. We're always going to apply this filter. And let's skip over the run method for right now and go down to the filterType. And this particular filter we're going to create a pre filter, so we can say

127

return pre. And then for the filterOrder, return 0 is okay, so we'll just leave that the same. In order to get access to the request to add headers to it, we need to get access to the RequestContext. So let's clear this TODO and say RequestContext ctx = RequestContext.getCurrentContext. And within the RequestContext there's the addZuulRequestHeader method. And image that our use case is to add the location of the incoming request, so we'll name this header x-location. And we're going to mock this; we'll say that every request comes from USA. And then last, remember that the return value is not actually used in the current implementation, so returning null is going to be okay for our purposes. Let's close this file and open up our main application class. And within our main application class, we'll annotate this with @Configuration.

```
package io.ajay.kumar;
import
org.springframework.boot.SpringApplication;
import
org.springframework.boot.autoconfigure.Spri
ngBootApplication;
import
org.springframework.cloud.client.discovery.E
nableDiscoveryClient;
import
org.springframework.cloud.netflix.zuul.Enabl
eZuulProxy;
import
org.springframework.context.annotation.Bean
;
import
org.springframework.context.annotation.Conf
iguration;
```

```
import
io.schultz.dustin.filters.AddRequestHeaderFilt
er;
@SpringBootApplication
@EnableZuulProxy
@EnableDiscoveryClient
@Configuration
public class GatewayServiceApplication {
public static void main(String[] args) {
 SpringApplication.run(GatewayServiceAppli
cation.class, args);
}
@Bean
public AddRequestHeaderFilter
addRequestHeaderFilter() {
 return new AddRequestHeaderFilter();
}
}
```

And then we're going to want to define the
AddRequestHeaderFilter as an @Bean here,
so we'll say public AddRequestHeaderFilter,
and we're going to return a new
AddRequestHeaderFilter. And again, make
sure we annotate this with @Bean. And that's
all the changes that we need to make to the
gateway-service, so let's go ahead and close
this and collapse the gateway-service. And
then let's go ahead and open up the hello-
service and open up the main application
class.

```
package io.ajay.kumar;
import
org.springframework.boot.SpringApplication;
import
org.springframework.boot.autoconfigure.Spri
ngBootApplication;
import
org.springframework.cloud.client.discovery.E
nableDiscoveryClient;
```

```
import
org.springframework.web.bind.annotation.Re
questHeader;
import
org.springframework.web.bind.annotation.Re
questMapping;
import
org.springframework.web.bind.annotation.Re
stController;
@SpringBootApplication
@EnableDiscoveryClient
@RestController
public class HelloServiceApplication {
public static void main(String[] args) {
 SpringApplication.run(HelloServiceApplicati
on.class, args);
}
@RequestMapping
public String hello(@RequestHeader("x-
location") String location) {
 return "Hello from " + location + "!";
}
}
```

In our handler method, we're going to add a
new parameter. We're going to say String
location. And we're going to annotate this with
@RequestHeader, and then we're going to
give it the name of that request header that
the gateway-service is adding to the request,
which is x-location. And then we'll modify the
string to say Hello from location, and go ahead
and save that. And that's all the changes that
we need to make to our application for this
demo. So we can go ahead and close this and
minimize the hello-service, and we're ready to
start things up. So we'll want to start the
discovery-server first. So expand the
discovery-server, locate the main application
class, right-click, Run As, Spring Boot App.

After that, we'll start the gateway-service, so collapse that and open the gateway-service, highlight the main application class, **Run As, Spring Boot App**. And then last, let's start up the hello-service. So collapse the gateway-service, head over to the hello-service, right-click, **Run As, Spring Boot App**. Next, start up your browser and visit localhost:8080/hello.

← → C   ⓘ localhost:8080/hello

Hello from USA!

And there we have it. We have the Hello and then we have the USA, which came from the gateway-service, which added it as a request header, which the hello-service then consumed and appended to it's Hello string to come out with the string Hello from USA!

Summary

We've now completed the module, so let's take a quick moment to recap what we've learned.

- The need for intelligent routing
- Gateway service
- Netflix Zuul

    - @EnableZuulProxy
    - Configuring routes
    - Writing filters

First, we looked at the reasons why Intelligent Routing is needed in the first place and why it's important. Then we looked at how routing is implemented via an API Gateway, or a gateway service. And last, we saw how we can use Netflix Zuul as a gateway service to route and filter our requests and responses to and from back-end services.

Module 6: Calling Services Using Client-side Load Balancing

Module Introduction

In this module we'll learn how to utilize client-side load balancing to distribute the workload of a service in a cloud-native application.

- Load balancing

    - Server-side
    - Client-side

- Netflix Ribbon

    - With & without service discovery

        - @Loadbalanced
        - @RibbonClient

    - Custom Ribbon configuration

We'll start off with what is load balancing, and what role does it play in a cloud-native application? Then we'll talk about traditional server-side load balancing, which you're probably already familiar with. Then we'll introduce client-side load balancing, what it is and how it differs from server-side load balancing. Next, we'll introduce Netflix Ribbon and how we can utilize it with Spring Cloud to implement client-side load balancing. We'll learn how to implement it with and without service discovery using two new annotations: the @LoadBalanced annotation and the @RibbonClient annotation. We'll finish off the module with a section on how to customize Ribbon's configuration for things like different load balancing algorithms or different ways to check the health of a service before sending a request to it.

Client-side vs. Server-side Load Balancing

So what is load balancing? Simply put, load balancing is a way to improve the distribution of workload across multiple computing resources. And you probably already knew that, so the more important question is what role does load balancing play in a cloud-native architecture? And the answer to that is actually a very important one, probably even more important than in a non-cloud-native architecture. And the reason for that becomes clearer when you look at the differences in the architecture. In a non-cloud-native application, you go from having multiple instances of a single application with a single load balancer to multiple services with multiple instances and multiple load balancers. And you can start to see the importance of a load balancer just by the sheer number of load balancers that we need in a cloud-native application. There are typically two different types of load balancers. There's the server-side load balancer where the server is responsible for the distribution of the load, and there's the client-side load balancer where the caller is responsible for the distribution of the load. Let's take a look at each of these in a bit more detail. With server-side load balancing, a request to another service doesn't go directly to the service itself and instead goes to a server in front of the service, which then decides which of the multiple instances it should forward the request to. With client-side load balancing, there is no intermediary. The client, or the caller of the service, is aware of all of the instances of a service via a known list or service discovery. And the client is then responsible for deciding which of the multiple instances it should send the request to. To solidify our understanding of server-side versus client-side load balancing, let's look at each of them side by side.

- Server-side

    - Server distributes requests
    - Hardware or software based
    - Extra hop
    - Various balancing algorithms support

- Occurs outside of the request process
- Centralized or distributed

- Client-side

  - Client distributes request
  - Software based
  - No extra hops
  - Various balancing algorithms support
  - Occurs within the request process
  - Typically distributed

With server-side load balancing, the server obviously distributes the request, and with client-side load balancing, the client obviously distributes the request. Server-side load balancing is typically hardware based, but it can also be software based. Client-side load balancing, on the other hand, is software based. You incur an extra hop with server-side load balancing since the request doesn't go directly to the service and has to go through an intermediary first. Whereas with client-side load balancing, you don't incur any extra hops once you know the location of the services. Both server-side and client-side load balancing have support for various load balancing algorithms. With server-side load balancing, the actual load balancing happens outside of the request process, whereas with client-side load balancing, the actual load balancing happens within the request process. And lastly, server-side load balancing can be either centralized or distributed, whereas client-side load balancing is typically distributed. Given all of these differences, it's clear that client-side load balancing is a natural fit for cloud-native architectures.

Getting Started with Spring Cloud and Netflix Ribbon

We've set the stage for client-side load balancing. Now let's talk about how to actually implement it with Spring Cloud. As I mentioned in the introduction to this module, we'll use a library called Netflix Ribbon to implement client-side load balancing. And Netflix Ribbon is an Inter Process Communication library that has built-in software load balancers. Spring Cloud adds full integration with Netflix Ribbon to Spring's RestTemplate class. And we'll go into detail about what this exactly means, but in essence our RestTemplate will now understand how to balance requests across multiple instances of a service. Spring Cloud also adds features that make it really easy to declare different types of load balancing algorithms and availability checks. Next, let's talk about how to use Spring Cloud and Netflix Ribbon. And before we get started, just a quick note. In each of these sections I'll explain all of the steps necessary to kind of get going, and then at the end we'll walk through a demo where you can follow along. Using Netflix Ribbon with Spring Cloud is extremely easy, just like all of the other Spring Cloud projects.
Using SpringCloud &Netflix Ribbon

pom.xml
```
<dependencyManagement>
  <dependencies>
    <dependency>

<groupId>org.springframework.cloud</groupId>
      <artifactId>spring-cloud-dependencies</artifactId>

<version>Camden.SR2</version><type>pom</type>
      <scope>import</scope></dependency>
  </dependencies>
</dependencyManagement>
```
In your dependencyManagement section of your pom.xml, define a new dependency on spring-cloud-dependencies.
```
<dependency>

<groupId>org.springframework.cloud</groupId>
  <artifactId>spring-cloud-starter-ribbon</artifactId>
</dependency>
```
And make sure that it's of type pom and has a scope of import. Still within your pom.xml, in the dependency section, define a new dependency on spring-cloud-starter-ribbon. Spring Cloud's Netflix Ribbon support adds two new annotations.

- Two New Annotations

  - @LoadBalanced : Marks a RestTemplate to support load balancing

- @RibbonClient : Used for custom configuration and when Service Discovery is absent

The first one is the @LoadBalanced annotation, and this annotation is used when you're creating a RestTemplate. And it's used to mark that that RestTemplate should be a load balanced RestTemplate as opposed to just a standard RestTemplate. The second annotation is the @RibbonClient annotation, and this annotation is mainly for configuration purposes. You would use it to configure a custom Ribbon client, as well as when you're not using service discovery to set up an actual Ribbon client. Let's look at how to use the @LoadBalanced annotation first.

Using the @LoadBalanced Annotation

It's really easy to get started and create a load balanced RestTemplate.
Creating a Load Balanced RestTemplate

```
@Configuration
public class MyConfiguration{
    @Bean
    @LoadBalanced
    public RestTemplate restTemplate(){
        return new RestTemplate();
    }
}
```

In your @Configuration class, you define a new method annotated with @Bean that returns a new RestTemplate. Then you annotate that same method with the

@LoadBalanced annotation. And what this does is it tells Spring that the RestTemplate should support load balancing. And what that means behind the scenes is that the RestTemplate that's returned will actually have an interceptor, a RestTemplate interceptor, that utilizes the Ribbon load balancer client to actually call our services and balance between the different instances. And, by default, it'll use a round-robin algorithm for distributing that load. Next, let's look at how you would actually use this load balanced RestTemplate if you were trying to call a service and you were using service discovery.

Using a Load Balanced RestTemplate With Service Discovery

Suppose my-service is the name of a service running on port 9000 at mycompany.com and is discoverable via Service Discovery. There are 2 instances running.

Instead of restTemplate.getForEntity("http://mycompany.com:9000/u/1",...) or restTemplate.getForEntity("http://128.168.10.10:9000/u/1",...)

Use RestTemplate like this instead restTemplate.getForEntity("http://my-service/u/1",...)

Suppose you had two instances of a service called my-service running on port 9000 on multiple servers at mycompany.com. And also suppose that my-service was discoverable via service discovery. Instead of passing the mycompany.com URL or IP address to the RestTemplate, you can actually pass a URL that uses a logical identifier to represent the service. In this case, we've used the logical identifier my-service. And this is the same name that the service is registered under at the Service Discovery Server. And at runtime the RestTemplate will function as the client-side load balancer. And it'll use service discovery to resolve the real location of the my-service instances and then use the configured load balancing algorithm to distribute the load between them.

Demo: Load Balancing Using Ribbon with Service Discovery

In this demo, we'll set up a Ribbon client that utilizes service discovery and balances requests between multiple instances of a service. Since we'll be using service discovery to locate the instances of the service, we'll need to have a Service Discovery Server set up. If you've been following along in the previous modules of the course, you should already have the discovery server set up within your IDE. Once you have the discovery server set up, we're ready to get started. Open up a browser and head over to start.spring.io. In the Group section, change this to io.ajay.kumar. And then for the name of the artifact, we're going to call this ribbon-time-service. In the Dependencies section, add the Web dependency and the Eureka Discovery dependency.

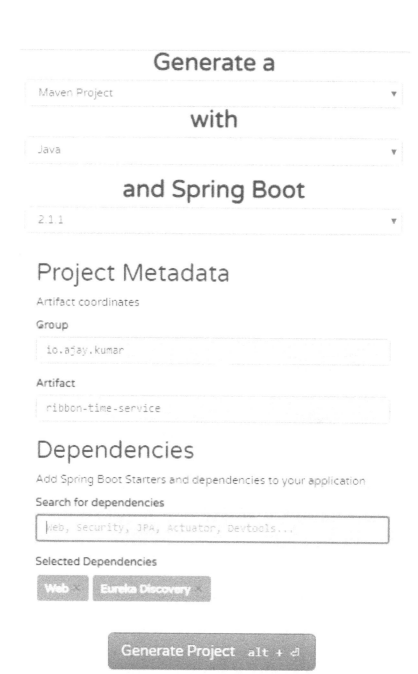

Generate a

Maven Project ▾

with

Java ▾

and Spring Boot

2.1.1 ▾

Project Metadata

Artifact coordinates

Group

io.ajay.kumar

Artifact

ribbon-time-service

Dependencies

Add Spring Boot Starters and dependencies to your application

Search for dependencies

Web, Security, JPA, Actuator, Devtools...

Selected Dependencies

Web ✕ Eureka Discovery ✕

Generate Project alt + ↵

Once you have everything filled out, click the Generate Project button, and it'll create and download a zip for you. Still on the SPRING INITIALIZR page, change the artifact name from ribbon-time-service to ribbon-tie-app.

Then, in the Dependencies section, add a new dependency on Ribbon.

Generate a

Maven Project ▾

with

Java ▾

and Spring Boot

2.1.1 ▾

Project Metadata

Artifact coordinates

Group

io.ajay.kumar

Artifact

ribbon-time-app

Dependencies

Add Spring Boot Starters and dependencies to your application

Search for dependencies

Web, Security, JPA, Actuator, Devtools...

Selected Dependencies

Web ×   Eureka Discovery ×   Ribbon ×

Generate Project   alt + ⏎

Again, once you have everything filled out, click the Generate Project button, and that'll create and download a zip for you. Unzip both

of those zip files and head back to your IDE. I've imported the ribbon-time-service and ribbon-time-app. Right-click on the empty area within the Package Explorer, go to Import, choose Existing Maven Projects, click Next, click Browse, browse to the location of the downloaded zip file, click Open, and click Finish. We'll work on the ribbon-time-service first, so expand the project and open up the main application class.

```
∨ ⬛ ribbon-time-service [boot]
   > 🗒 Spring Elements
   ∨ 🗁 src/main/java
      ∨ ⊞ io.ajay.kumar.ribbontimeservice
         > 🗎 RibbonTimeServiceApplication.java
   > 🗁 src/main/resources
   > 🗁 src/test/java
   > ▦ JRE System Library [JavaSE-1.8]
   > ▦ Maven Dependencies
   > 🗁 src
   > 🗁 target
     🗎 mvnw
     🗎 mvnw.cmd
     Ⓜ pom.xml
```

Within the main application class, add two annotations, the @RestController annotation and the @EnableDiscoveryClient annotation. package io.ajay.kumar.ribbontimeservice; import java.util.Date; import org.springframework.beans.factory.annotation.Value; import org.springframework.boot.SpringApplication; import org.springframework.boot.autoconfigure.SpringBootApplication;

```
import
org.springframework.cloud.client.discovery.E
nableDiscoveryClient;
import
org.springframework.web.bind.annotation.Ge
tMapping;
import
org.springframework.web.bind.annotation.Re
stController;
@RestController
@EnableDiscoveryClient
@SpringBootApplication
public class RibbonTimeServiceApplication {
    @Value("${server.port}")
    private int port;
    public static void main(String[] args) {
        SpringApplication.run(RibbonTime
ServiceApplication.class, args);
    }
    @GetMapping
    public String getTime() {
        return "The current time is "+ new
Date().toString()
                    +"(answered by service
running on "+port+")";
    }
}
```

Then we need to add one request handler
method, so hit Return a few times and do
public String getTime. And we'll annotate that
with a shortcut version @GetMapping, which
is just a request mapping that's a GET. Then
in the body of the method we'll return The
current time is, and we'll construct a new Date
object and turn that into a string. For
demonstration purposes, we're going to want
to know which instance is responding to the
request. And currently we have no way of
telling. We wouldn't be able to tell one from

144

the other. So we're going to make one addition to the response. So we're going to say + answered by service running on, and then we'll have a port variable, and then we'll close that parenthesis. And since each of our services has to be running on a different port, we can tell each one of them apart. So let's make sure that we actually define that port variable. Come up here and add a private int port, and then we'll annotate this with @Value annotation. And we'll inject this with the server.port variable. And before we fire this up, we need to configure a few properties within our application.properties. So go ahead and close that and open up src/main/resources and open up the application.properties file. application.properties spring.application.name=time-service eureka.client.service-url.defaultZone=http://localhost:8761/eureka In the application.properties, we're going to set two properties. The first one is the spring.application.name property, and we're going to set that to time-service. And the second property we'll set is to configure the location of the Service Discovery Server, so eureka.client.service-url.defaultZone. And then we'll set that to localhost:8761/eureka. We now have everything we need to start the ribbon time-service, so we can go ahead and close this and minimize this. And the first thing we'll want to do is start the discovery server. So expand the discovery-server project and navigate to the main application class. Right-click on the main application class, and go Run As, Spring Boot App. Go ahead and minimize the discovery-server and expand the ribbon-time-service, and navigate to the main application class, right-click on it, and go to

Run As, and then choose Run Configurations. Since we're starting up two instances of the ribbon-time-service, we need to configure two different run configurations. So if you come up here to the New launch configuration button, click that, and it'll create a new run configuration for you. We'll rename this to ribbon-time-service-1. And then for the Project, we'll make sure that we choose the ribbon-time-service, and for the Main type, hit Search and locate the RibbonTimeServiceApplication. In the Override properties section, we'll set the server.port, and we'll set that to 4444. And click Apply, and then we're going to duplicate this configuration and change the server port from all 4s to all 5s. So come up here to the Duplicate configuration button, click that, change the name from ribbon-time-service-1 to -2, and change the port from all 4s to all 5s. Once you've got everything configured, you can highlight the ribbon-time-service-1 and click Run. And then for the second instance, right-click on the main application class, go to Run As, locate Run Configurations, highlight the ribbon-time-service-2, and click Run. Just to make sure everything's running correctly, open up a browser and visit localhost:4444.

← → C ⓘ localhost:4444

The current time is Sun Dec 23 00:42:08 IST 2018(answered by service running on 444

And do the same, but change those 4s to all 5s.

← → C ⓘ localhost:5555

The current time is Sun Dec 23 00:42:47 IST 2018(answered by service running on 555

You should get a response from each of the services with the current time and then the current time and answered by service and whatever the respective port is. We can also quickly check that each of the services registered itself with the Service Discovery Server. So open up a new tab and visit localhost:8761.

spring Eureka

≡

System Status

Environment	test
Data center	default

Current time	2018-12-23T00:33:34 +0530
Uptime	00:06
Lease expiration enabled	false
Renews threshold	5
Renews (last min)	0

**EMERGENCY! EUREKA MAY BE INCORRECTLY CLAIMING INSTANCES ARE
UP WHEN THEY'RE NOT. RENEWALS ARE LESSER THAN THRESHOLD
AND HENCE THE INSTANCES ARE NOT BEING EXPIRED JUST TO BE SAFE.**

DS Replicas

localhost

Instances currently registered with Eureka

Application	AMIs	Availability Zones	Status
TIME-SERVICE	n/a (2)	(2)	UP (2) - DESKTOP-OIHU6JB:time-service:4444 , DESKTOP-OIHU6JB:time-service:5555

General Info

Name	Value
total-avail-memory	332mb
environment	test
num-of-cpus	4
current-memory-usage	221mb (66%)
server-uptime	00:06
registered-replicas	http://localhost:8761/eureka/
unavailable-replicas	http://localhost:8761/eureka/,
available-replicas	

Instance Info

Name	Value
ipAddr	192.168.29.2

148

If you scroll down under the heading Instances currently registered with Eureka, you'll see the application TIME-SERVICE, and you'll see that there are two instances. They're both UP. One of them is running on all 5s and another is running on all 4s. And we're back within the IDE, and so far all we've done is we've set up multiple instances of the ribbon-time-service and had each of them register with the Service Discovery Server. We're now ready to start developing the piece where we'll use Ribbon to load balance between each of the instances of the ribbon-time-service. In the Package Explorer under the ribbon-time-app, expand it and navigate to the main application class. Go ahead and expand the main application class just to give us a little bit more room. Just like we did with the ribbon-time-service, we'll add two annotations: first, the @RestController annotation, and second, the @EnableDiscoveryClient annotation. Next we'll inject a RestTemplate, so private RestTemplate, and make sure you annotate it with @Inject. And there's nothing right now that's providing this RestTemplate, so we're going to create a method that will return that new RestTemplate as a load balance RestTemplate. So if you come down here below the main, do public RestTemplate. Then within the body of the method, you're going to return new RestTemplate. And then annotate this with @Bean and @LoadBalanced. Now we need one more method, and that's the RequestMapping method, to actually handle the request for our ribbon-time-app. So come up here and do public String getTime, and we'll annotate this with the shortcut mapping again, so @GetMapping. And then within the

149

body of the method, we're going to use the RestTemplate to call our time-service and return the result. So we'll say return restTemplate.getForEntity. And then we'll say http://, and remember we use a logical identifier here, so we'll say time-service. And we'll say that the return type is a string and then make sure that we call getBody on the response. We're now ready to start up our ribbon-time-app and give it a run. So let's unmaximize this and right-click on the main application class, go to Run As, and choose Spring Boot App. Next, fire up a browser and visit localhost:8080.

The current time is Sun Dec 23 00:55:24 IST 2018(answered by service running on 4444

And you can see the response from the service running with the port on all 4s. And if we refresh that, we'll see the one running on the port with all 5s.

The current time is Sun Dec 23 00:56:15 IST 2018(answered by service running on 5555

And we can continue to refresh that, and we'll see that it alternates between each of the instances in a round-robin fashion.

Using the @RibbonClient Annotation

Now let's take a look at the other annotation, the @RibbonClient annotation. First we'll see how to use this annotation along with the @LoadBalanced annotation to achieve client-side load balancing without service discovery. @Configuration

```
@RibbonClient(name="someservice")
public class MyConfiguration{
...
}
```

In your @Configuration class, define the @RibbonClient annotation and set the name element to a meaningful value. You'll actually refer to this value in the configuration, as well as the URL of the RestTemplate.

```
application.properties
<ribbon_client_name>.ribbon.eureka.enabled
=false
<ribbon_client_name>.ribbon.listOfServers=h
ttp://host:9000, http://host:9001
```

OR

```
application.yml
<ribbon_client_name>:ribbon:eureka:enabled
: false
listOfServers=http://host:9000,
http://host:9001
```

* Replace <ribbon_client_name> with the name field value of @RibbonClient

Then, in your application.properties or your application.yml, define two new properties. And remember the name element that we set on the @RibbonClient annotation. You'll prefix each of your properties with that value. So the first property, the ribbon_client_name.ribbon.eureka.enabled=false, tells Ribbon to disable service discovery support. The next property, the ribbon_client_name.ribbon.listOfServers, is a comma-separated list of URLs that Ribbon should use to distribute the requests among. And in this case, we've set the different URLs to two different addresses, one running on port 9000 and the other running on port 9001.

```
restTemplate.getForEntity("http://someservic
e/",...)
```

Once you have everything configured, you can use the RestTemplate just like you did with service discovery. Except this time instead of calling the service name, you use the value of the name element that you set up in the @RibbonClient annotation.

Demo: Load Balancing Using Ribbon Without Service Discovery

In this demo, we'll learn how to utilize the Ribbon client without service discovery. Now, we're going to build on the previous demo that we did utilizing service discovery as each of the demos share a lot in common. The first thing we'll do is expand the ribbon-time-service and open up the main application class. In the main application class, remove the @EnableDiscoveryClient annotation.
package io.ajay.kumar.ribbontimeservice;
import java.util.Date;
import org.springframework.beans.factory.annotation.Value;
import org.springframework.boot.SpringApplication;
import org.springframework.boot.autoconfigure.SpringBootApplication;
import org.springframework.cloud.client.discovery.EnableDiscoveryClient;
import org.springframework.web.bind.annotation.GetMapping;

```
import
org.springframework.web.bind.annotation.Re
stController;
@RestController
@SpringBootApplication
public class RibbonTimeServiceApplication {
    @Value("${server.port}")
    private int port;
    public static void main(String[] args) {
        SpringApplication.run(RibbonTime
ServiceApplication.class, args);
    }
    @GetMapping
    public String getTime() {
        return "The current time is "+ new
Date().toString()
                    +"(answered by service
running on "+port+")";
    }
}
```

Go ahead and close that, and open up the src/main/resources application.properties, and delete the property that sets the location of the Service Discovery Server.

application.properties
spring.application.name=time-service

Once you've got the property deleted, go ahead and close that. And we're now ready to start up the ribbon-time-service without service discovery. If you come up to the green Play button and click the little drop-down caret, you'll see that we have all of our run configurations that we've use in the past. So we'll want to use each of these ribbon-time-services to start each of the instances. So we'll start ribbon-time-service-1, and then we'll start ribbon-time-service-2. Just to make sure that our ribbon-time-service instances started up correctly, let's do a quick sanity check. So visit localhost:4444, and it's running there. And then open up a New Tab and visit localhost:5555, and it's running there. So everything with our ribbon-time-service is good to go. Next, we'll minimize the ribbon-time-service project and open up the ribbon-time-app. And once you've opened it, navigate to the main application class.

```
@RestController
@RibbonClient(name="time-service")
@SpringBootApplication
public class RibbonTimeAppApplication {
    @Inject
    private RestTemplate restTemplate;
    public static void main(String[] args) {
        SpringApplication.run(RibbonTime
AppApplication.class, args);
    }
    @GetMapping
    public String getTime() {
        return
restTemplate.getForEntity("http://time-
service", String.class).getBody();
    }
    @Bean
    @LoadBalanced
    public RestTemplate restTemplate() {
        return new RestTemplate();
    }
}
```

And just like we did with the ribbon-time-service, we'll want to delete this @EnableDiscoveryClient. Now we're going to add a new annotation, the @RibbonClient annotation, and we're going to set the name element to the time-service string. And this is the same time-service that we used when we were using service discovery, and we'll use it in pretty much the same fashion. We'll refer to it in the RestTemplate URL as a logical service identifier, and then configure what those particular instances are that represent that service within configuration. Let's go ahead and close this and open up our src/main/resources and our application.properties.

application.properties
time-service.ribbon.eureka.enabled=false
time-service.ribbon.listOfServers=http://host:4444, http://host:5555

In our application.properties, we'll prefix all of the properties that we're setting up to configure our Ribbon client with the name of the Ribbon client. In our case, we use time-service. So we'll say time-service-ribbon-eureka-enabled=false. And this is the property that'll tell Ribbon not to use service discovery. So we have one more property to set, so we'll say time-service.ribbon.listOfServers. And we'll set this to a comma-separated list of the location of all of the instances of our time-service. So we have http://localhost:4444, and then we have that exact same one except for it's all 5s. And that's all the configuration we need to get set up, so we can go ahead and close this. And we can go over to our main application class, right-click on it, go to Run As, and choose Spring Boot App. Next, go ahead and fire up a browser and visit localhost:8080.

← → C ⓘ localhost:8080

The current time is Sun Dec 23 00:55:24 IST 2018(answered by service running on 4444)

And you can see that we got a response from the service running on the port with all 4s. And if we refresh that, we'll see that we get a response from the one on all 5s.

And we can continue to refresh that and see that it round-robins between each of the instances of the time-service.

Customizing Your RibbonClient Configuration: Introduction

In this last section, we'll learn how to customize an individual Ribbon client using declarative configuration. And what this will allow us to do is define custom configuration that applies to a specific Ribbon client instead of to all Ribbon clients. And what that buys us is it allows us to define different client-side load balancing behavior for different services.
@Configuration
@RibbonClient(
name="otherservice",
configuration=OtherServiceConfig.class)
public class MyConfiguration{
...
}
 In your @Configuration class, define the @RibbonClient annotation and set the name element just like we did when we configured the previous Ribbon client. This time though, you'll define an additional configuration element, and you'll set that to another @Configuration class.
package io.ajay.config.kumar;
//Different package so it is not picked up by
@ComponentScan
@Configuration
public class OtherServiceConfig {

}

This additional @Configuration class will contain all of the custom configuration for a specific Ribbon client. And that configuration is defined by methods that are annotated with the @Bean annotation. So this configuration is just like any other @Configuration class. There's nothing special about it. You would just configure your @Beans just like you do normally. But since this configuration only pertains to a specific Ribbon client, it shouldn't be subject to any sort of component scanning. If it were, the configuration that was defined in that @Configuration class would end up applying to all Ribbon clients instead of just a specific Ribbon client.

```
@Configuration
public class OtherServiceConfig {
        @Bean
        public <bean_type>
        <method_name>(){...}
}
```

Default Ribbon Client @Beans

Replace <bean_type> and <method_name> with values to override:

http://cloud.spring.io/spring-cloud-static/Camden.SR6/#_customizing_the_ribbon_client

Most likely to be customized: IRule & IPing

There are a number of different classes that are needed to set up a Ribbon client, and by default Spring Cloud defines those as @Beans and then allows you to override any of them for custom configuration. Let's take a look at the Spring Cloud documentation to see what @Beans you can override.

I've loaded up the Spring Cloud documentation, and we're looking at a number of different beans that are required to set up a Ribbon client. And for the most part, you typically won't need to override any of these with the exception of two of the beans. That's the IRule bean and the IPing bean. The IRule bean controls the load balancing algorithm, and the IPing bean controls the availability checks on the instances that are being load balanced. Let's take a look at each of these beans in a bit more detail.

Customizing Your RibbonClient Configuration: The IRule Bean

As I mentioned, the IRule bean is used to control the load balancing strategy that's used to balance the distribution of workload between the instances that are being load balanced. You can choose to create your own custom IRule implementation, or you can choose from one of the several different defaults. Let's talk about a few of our available options.

- IRuleImplementations

    - RoundRobinRule
    - ResponseTimeWeightedRule
    - RandomRule
    - ZoneAvoidanceRule

There's the RoundRobinRule implementation, which is just like it sounds, an implementation of the round-robin balancing algorithm, which distributes the workload evenly among all instances. There's the ResponseTimeWeightedRule implementation, which is also a round-robin algorithm, but it dynamically assigns weights based on the average response time from each of the instances. There's the RandomRule implementation, which simply picks an instance to send traffic to at random. And there's the ZoneAvoidanceRule, which is also a round-robin algorithm implementation; however, it filters out servers to send traffic to based on the AWS zone and availability. Let's look at an example to make this a bit more concrete.

```
@Configuration
public class OtherServiceConfig{
    @Bean
    public IRule ribbonRule(){
    return new RoundRobinRule();
}
}
```

If, for instance, we wanted to override the default IRule to use the RoundRobinRule implementation, we'd define a new method annotated with the @Bean annotation, and we'd return a new RoundRobinRule.

Customizing Your RibbonClient Configuration: The IPing Bean

The IPing bean is responsible for choosing the strategy to check the liveliness or the availability of a given instance that's being load balanced. Just like the IRule bean, you can also implement your own custom IPing implementations, or you can choose from one of the several different defaults. Let's take a look at what's available.

- **IPingImplementations**

  - **DummyPing**
  - **PingUrl**
  - **NIWSDiscoveryPing**

There's the DummyPing implementation, which is just as dumb as it sounds. It's simply always returning true when it's asked about the liveliness of a service. You'd use this if you simply don't care to check the liveliness or the availability and you always want to send traffic to all of the instances regardless. There's the PingUrl implementation, which is an implementation that allows you to set an expected response and then makes an actual HTTP call to the service and checks the result. So you'd typically point this at something like the service's health check URL. And then there's the DiscoveryPing implementation, which would be something that would be automatically configured for you if you were using something like Eureka service discovery. And what this would do is it would just consult with the discovery client to determine the liveliness of any particular instance. Again, let's look at an example to make this a bit more concrete.

IPing: Liveliness Check

```
@Configuration
public class OtherServiceConfig{
  @Bean
  public IPing ribbonPing(){
  PingUrl pingUrl=new PingUrl();
  pingUrl.setExpectedContent("true");
  return pingUrl;
}
```

}
So just like we did with the IRule implementation, you would define a new method annotated with the @Bean annotation, and then you return the implementation of your choice. So in this case, we're going to return a PingUrl. So we create a new instance of the PingUrl, we set the expected content to true, and then return that instance.

Demo: Customizing the RibbonClient Load Balancing Strategy

In this demo, we'll learn how to customize our Ribbon client that we're using to call the ribbon-time-service. And again, we're going to be building on the previous demo. So make sure that you've completed the demo where you set up a Ribbon client without using service discovery. The first thing we'll do is we'll come up here to the green Play button and start each of the instances of the ribbon-time-service. Both of the ribbon-time-service instances are started. Now remember, in order to create custom configuration for a Ribbon client, we need to create our own @Configuration class. Let's open the ribbon-time-app project and create a new package. So right-click, New, and come here to Package. And we're actually going to rename this from io.ajay.kumar to io.ajay.config.kumar. Remember that we want to have a different package name so that the @Configuration class isn't subject to component scanning;

otherwise, it would apply to all of our Ribbon clients. In the new package, right-click and go to New and choose Class. And we'll call this our RibbonTimeConfig class. Go ahead and click Finish.

```
package io.ajay.config.kumar;
import
org.springframework.context.annotation.Bean
;
import
org.springframework.context.annotation.Conf
iguration;
import com.netflix.loadbalancer.IRule;
import
com.netflix.loadbalancer.RandomRule;
@Configuration
public class RibbonTimeConfig {
@Bean
public IRule ribbonRule() {
 return new RandomRule();
}
}
```

Then we're going to annotate this class, of course, with @Configuration. And then for this demo, we're going to customize the load balancing strategy. So we'll come down here and we'll define a new IRule. So we'll say public IRule, and we'll call this ribbonRule. And then in the body of the method, we'll say return new RandomRule. And what this will do is it'll pick a random instance to send traffic to as opposed to what we were using before where we were evenly balancing between each of the instances. And last, make sure that we don't forget to add the @Bean annotation to our method. We're done with our custom configuration, so we can go ahead and close that. And then we can open up the main RibbonTimeApplication.

```java
@RestController
@RibbonClient(name = "time-service",
configuration=RibbonTimeConfig.class)
@SpringBootApplication
public class RibbonTimeAppApplication {
@Inject
private RestTemplate restTemplate;
public static void main(String[] args) {
 SpringApplication.run(RibbonTimeAppAppli
cation.class, args);
}
@GetMapping
public String getTime() {
 return
restTemplate.getForEntity("http://time-
service", String.class).getBody();
}
@Bean
@LoadBalanced
public RestTemplate restTemplate() {
 return new RestTemplate();
}
}
```

And on the RibbonClient annotation, add a new configuration element, and set it to the custom configuration class that we set up, the RibbonTimeConfig class. We're now ready to start up our application and try out our custom configuration. So go ahead and close this and right-click on the main application class, go to Run As, and choose Spring Boot App. Go ahead and fire up a browser and visit localhost:8080.

And, as you can see, we got a response from the instance running with the port that's all 5s.

And if we refresh that, we'll see that we get an instance with all 4s.

← → C   www.localhost:8080

The current time is Mon Feb 27 11:09:08 MDT 2018(answered by service running on 4444)

But if we continue to refresh it, we'll see that it doesn't evenly balance between each of the instances like it did before and instead picks them at a random interval.

Summary

We're at the end of this module, so let's quickly go over what we learned.

- **Differences between client-side & server-side load balancing**
- **Netflix Ribbon**

  - **@LoadBalanced & @RibbonClient**

    - **With & without service discovery**

  - **Custom Ribbon client configuration**

We first talked about what is load balancing and what are the differences between client-side load balancing and server-side load balancing. Then we introduced the Netflix Ribbon project and learned how to use the @LoadBalanced and the @RibbonClient annotations to set up client-side load balancing with and without service discovery. In the last section, we saw how we could use

the @RibbonClient annotation with a separate @Configuration class to set up custom configuration for a specific Ribbon client.

Module 7: Creating Self-healing Services with Circuit Breaker

Introduction

In this module we'll learn how to develop services in a cloud-native architecture that are both fault tolerant and self-healing.
- Failures in a distributed system
  - Cascading failures
  - Circuit breaker pattern
- Netflix Hystrix project
  - @EnableCircuitBreaker
  - @HystrixCommand
- Hystrix Dashboard
  - @EnableHystrixDashboard
  - Turbine to aggregate Hystrix streams
    - @EnableTurbine

We'll begin the module with a short section on failures in a cloud-native or distributed system. We'll look at why failures are more prevalent and understand a common side effect called cascading failures. Then we'll introduce and understand the Circuit Breaker pattern and learn how it can help us build more fault-tolerant services. Next, we'll dive into Netflix Hystrix, which is a fault-tolerance library that, among other things, implements the Circuit Breaker pattern. We'll see how Spring Cloud makes it easy to get started with the @EnableCircuitBreaker annotation, and then we'll understand how to use the @HystrixCommand annotation to implement the Circuit Breaker pattern in our own services. We'll finish the module out by looking at one of the really nice features of Hystrix called the Hystrix Dashboard. We'll see how to enable it, how metrics are collected, how to interpret those results, and how to aggregate those results using another project from Netflix called Turbine.

Cascading Failures and Resource Overloading

In a distributed system, if there's anything that we can be 100% sure about, that's that failure is inevitable. But why though? Well, failure can happen at many different levels in a system.

- A Few Areas That Might Fail
    - Hardware fails
    - Networks fail
    - Software fails

Hardware can fail, networks can fail, and software can definitely fail. And a distributed system is no different in that sense, but the likelihood for failure is just simply much greater. You have more hardware, you have more network, and you have more software. And with these increased numbers comes that increased probability for failure. Adding to that chance of failure is the way in which processes communicate in a distributed system. Process communication that was once within a process is now done across a network. And even as resilient as our networks are today, there's still a much more likely chance of a communication failure across a network versus within a process. A particularly bad side effect of failures in a distributed system is something called a cascading failure. A cascading failure is a failure in a system in which a failure in one system can cascade, almost like dominos, to other parts of the system causing them to fail as well. To make this a bit more concrete, imagine that you have three services, Service A, Service B, and Service C. Service A calls Service B, and Service B calls Service C. And imagine that Service C runs out of memory and is very slow to serve requests to Service B. And even though Service B may have a timeout set up for calling Service C, if enough requests stack up against Service B, which require the use of Service C at a fast enough rate, resources at Service B will be entirely consumed before that timeout is ever reached, which in turn will cause Service B to fail. This same problem can happen all the way up the chain.

- Multiple issues at play
  - Fault tolerance problem
  - Resource overloading problem

There are multiple issues at play here. First, we have a fault tolerance problem. Calling services are unaware that the service that they're calling is likely to fail and yet they still attempt to call the service. And second, we have a resource overloading problem. Calling services are allowed to invoke dependent services with pretty much unconstrained resources.

Embracing Failure with the Circuit Breaker Pattern

- **Learn to embrace failure**
  - **Tolerate failures**
  - **Gracefully degrade**
- **Limit resources consumed**
  - **Constrain usage**

So how do we solve this problem of cascading failures and failures in general in a distributed system? Well, we have to learn to embrace and tolerate failures and degrade gracefully when we do. So in the event that a downstream dependent service is failing, it's actually better for the caller not to attempt to make a call to the dependent service, which is likely to fail. And instead, the caller should fail fast or degrade gracefully, perhaps by returning old data or empty results, and allow the failing service to recover. And then periodically check if the service has recovered. And, in turn, what this does is it relieves pressure from any upstream services that are waiting for a response. And the other thing that we need to do is we need to limit the resources that are consumed. So clients should put limits on the number of resources allowed to call a dependent service. And what this does is it prevents those requests from stacking up unconstrained, which could cause the client to fail itself. The first strategy for fault tolerance is actually a well-known pattern, so much so that it has its own name. And it's called the Circuit Breaker pattern. And the Circuit Breaker pattern is a design pattern in modern software used to detect failures and encapsulate the logic of preventing those failures from reoccurring constantly. The name Circuit Breaker comes from the idea that the pattern shares a lot of similarities with how a real circuit breaker works. And you may or may not be familiar with what a circuit breaker is, so let me quickly explain. A circuit breaker is a switch that prevents too much current from flowing through a circuit. And if too much current flows through a circuit, it could cause damage or even start things on fire. And what the circuit breaker does is it prevents that by opening the circuit when it detects that there's too much current flowing through it. And you most likely have something like this in your residence to prevent your circuits from becoming overloaded. And, if you notice, all of the switches are flipped down, and thus all of the circuits are closed. Suppose you accidently overload the rightmost circuit by plugging in a device that consumes a lot of power. And the circuit breaker would detect this and break the circuit, or open it, and prevent any additional current from flowing through it. And you can see switch is flipped up indicating that the circuit has been broken and there is no more current flowing through it. By now, I'm sure you can see the common theme between a real circuit breaker and the Circuit Breaker pattern. Both are meant to detect and prevent failures that might damage other components.

Fault Tolerance with Netflix Hystrix and Spring Cloud

Spring Cloud implements fault tolerance with the help of a library from Netflix called Netflix Hystrix. Hystrix is a latency and fault-tolerance library, and it was designed to stop cascading failures and enable resiliency in distributed systems.

- Implements the circuit breaker pattern
  - Wraps calls and watches for failures
    - 10 sec rolling window
    - 20 request volume
    - >= 50% error rate
  - Waits & tries a single request after 5 sec
  - Fallbacks
- Protects services from being overloaded
  - Thread pools, semaphores, & cascading failures

It's a concrete implementation of the Circuit Breaker pattern, and it allows you to easily wrap calls and automatically watches them for failures that meet a certain volume and air-percentage threshold within a given rolling window. The default for the rolling window is 10 seconds, and the request volume must be at least 20 requests. And if 50% or more of the requests are errors, then the circuit will be tripped and no requests will be allowed through. So if for instance you had a thousand requests in a 10 second window, if 500 of them were errors, then the circuit would be tripped. Hystrix will periodically recheck if the circuit should be closed, and it does that by allowing a single request through every 5 seconds. That's the default. And if that request succeeds, then it will close the circuit, and if it fails, then it will remain open. Any requests that are short-circuited or timed-out or rejected or failed will be given a chance to execute what's called a fallback method. And, as I mentioned before, a fallback might be something like returning cache data, a default value, or just something like an empty response. In addition to the Circuit Breaker pattern, Hystrix also has additional functionality that protects services from being overloaded. All Hystrix wrap calls are bounded either by a thread pool or a semaphore. And what this does is it constrains the resource usage, like we talked about earlier, so that requests don't stack up and consume all of the valuable resources. And in the event that all of the available resources are consumed, any new requests will fail immediately and execute the fallback method, if one is available.

Using Spring Cloud and Netflix Hystrix

Using Spring Cloud and Netflix Hystrix is extremely easy. And before we dive in, just a quick note. I'll explain all the steps necessary to get going and then walk you through a demo at the end where you can kind of follow along. I'll follow that pattern throughout the remainder of this module, so just keep that in mind.

```
pom.xml
<dependencyManagement>
  <dependencies>
    <dependency>
      <groupId>org.springframework.cloud
</groupId>
      <artifactId>spring-cloud-
dependencies</artifactId>
      <version>Camden.SR2</version>
      <type>pom</type>
      <scope>import</scope>
    </dependency>
  </dependencies>
</dependencyManagement>
```

Just like you use all of the other Spring Cloud projects, you start by including a dependency in the dependencyManagement section of your pom.xml on spring-cloud-dependencies. And, as always, make sure that it's of type pom and has a scope of import.

```
<dependency>

<groupId>org.springframework.cloud</groupId>
    <artifactId>spring-cloud-starter-
hystrix</artifactId>
</dependency>
<dependency>

<groupId>org.springframework.boot</groupId>
    <artifactId>spring-boot-
actuator</artifactId>
</dependency>
```

Then, still within your pom.xml, within the dependency section, define a new dependency on spring-cloud-starter-hystrix. And if you'd like to be able to consume metrics for your

Hystrix calls, you'll also need to include a dependency on the spring-boot-actuator.

```
@SpringBootApplication
@EnableCircuitBreaker
public class Application{
   public static void main(String[]args){

SpringApplication.run(Application.class,args)
;
   }
}
```

In your main Application class, you define a new annotation, and that's the @EnableCircuitBreaker annotation.

```
@Service
public class Service{
      @HystrixCommand(fallbackMethod-"
somethingElse")
      public void doSomething(){
            ...
      }
      public void somethingElse(){
            ...
      }
}
```

And then in either your @Component or your @Service class, locate the method that you want to wrap with Hystrix, in our case this will be a method called doSomething, and annotate that method with the @HystrixCommand. Then, on the @HystrixCommand annotation, define a new attribute called fallbackMethod, and set that to the name of the method that you want to fall back to in the event of a failure. In terms of code, that's all there is to it.

- Be careful with Hystrix timeouts
  - Ensure timeouts encompass caller timeouts plus any retries

- **Default: 1000ms**
- **hystrix.command.default.execut ion.isolation.thread.timeoutInM illiseconds=<timeout_ms>**

But there's a gotcha that you have to look out for, and that's around the Hystrix timeout. And you need to make sure that your Hystrix timeouts encompass the caller timeouts plus any of the retries and then a little bit of a buffer. And the default timeout is set to 1000ms or a second, and if you need to change it, you can use this big, long property to set the timeout in milliseconds.

Demo: Implementing Fault Tolerance with Netflix Hystrix

In this demo, we'll build a simple weather service that returns a random weather condition, and then we'll use that in another app called the weather app that consumes that service. And in the weather app we'll protect our call to the weather service with Hystrix and implement a fallback for when the weather service is down or not responding. We'll be using service discovery to locate the weather service from our weather app, so make sure that you have the Service Discovery Server set up within your IDE. And if you've been following along throughout the course, you should already have this set up. Go ahead and open up a browser and head over to start.spring.io. In the Group section, change the group to io.ajay.kumar, and then for the name of the artifact, name it weather-service. In the Dependencies section, add the Web

dependency and the Eureka Discovery dependency.

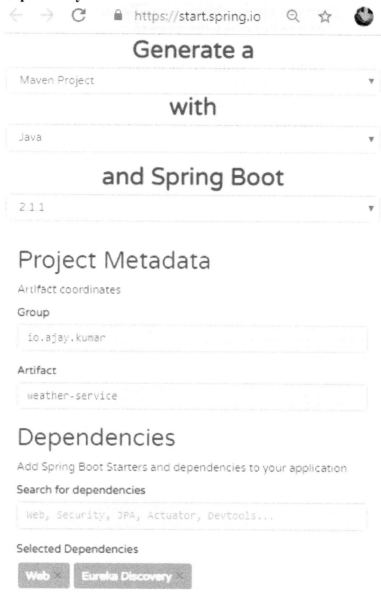

Once you have everything filled out, go ahead and click the Generate Project button, and it'll create and download a zip file for you. We're also going to use this page to generate the weather app project, so still on this page change the name of the artifact from weather-service to weather-app. Then in the Dependencies section, add the Hystrix dependency and the Actuator dependency.

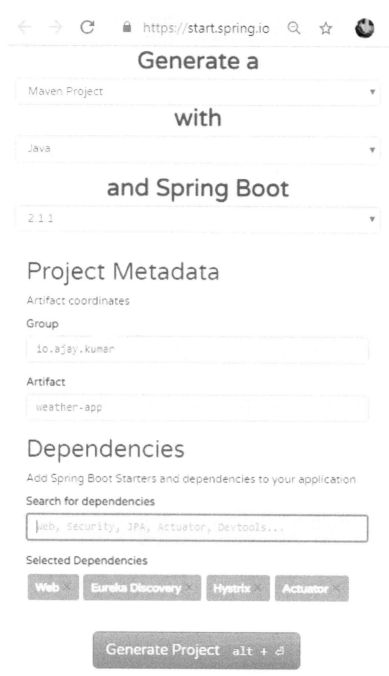

Again, once you have everything filled out, go ahead and click the Generate Project button, and it'll create and download that zip file for you. Go ahead and unzip both of those zip files and head back to your IDE. Back within your IDE, right-click on the empty space and choose Import, choose Existing Maven Projects, click Next, browse to the location of your downloaded zip file, and click Finish. Once you have the weather service imported, repeat the same process for the weather app. I have both projects imported into the IDE.

```
v  ᴹ⁵  weather-service [boot]
   >  📁  Spring Elements
   v  📁  src/main/java
      v  ⊞  io.ajay.kumar.weatherservice
         v  [J]  WeatherServiceApplication.java
            >  Q  WeatherServiceApplication
   >  📁  src/main/resources
   >  📁  src/test/java
   >  📚  JRE System Library [JavaSE-1.8]
   >  📚  Maven Dependencies
   >  📂  src
   >  📂  target
      📄  mvnw
      📄  mvnw.cmd
      ⓜ  pom.xml
```

We'll start by developing the weather service first, so go ahead and expand the weather-service and navigate to the main application class.
package io.ajay.kumar.weatherservice;
import
java.util.concurrent.ThreadLocalRandom;
import
org.springframework.boot.SpringApplication;
import
org.springframework.boot.autoconfigure.Spri
ngBootApplication;
import
org.springframework.cloud.client.discovery.E
nableDiscoveryClient;

```java
import
org.springframework.web.bind.annotation.Ge
tMapping;
import
org.springframework.web.bind.annotation.Re
stController;
@SpringBootApplication
@RestController
@EnableDiscoveryClient
public class WeatherServiceApplication {
    private String[] weather = new String[] {
"sunny", "cloudy", "rainy", "windy" };
    public static void main(String[] args) {
        SpringApplication.run(WeatherServ
iceApplication.class, args);
    }
    @GetMapping("/weather")
    public String getWeather() {
        int rand =
ThreadLocalRandom.current().nextInt(0, 4);
        return weather[rand];
    }
}
```

In the main application class, define two new
annotations, the @RestController annotation
and the @EnableDiscoveryClient annotation.
Then, at the top of the class, define a new
string array, so private String array. Go
ahead and call it weather, and then we're
going to set that to four different values.
We're going to say sunny, cloudy, rainy, and
windy. Next, we'll go ahead and define a
getWeather method. So come to the bottom
here and type public String getWeather. And
this will be our handler method, so let's go
ahead and annotate this with @GetMapping.
And we'll set the URL to /weather. In the body
of the method, we'll choose a random number
before 0 and 4 exclusive, and then we'll use

that to pick a random weather value. So we'll say int rand = ThreadLocalRandom.current.nextInt and give that a bound from 0 to 4. And then next, we'll return weather of rand to pick a random weather value. And that's all we have for the coding part of our weather service. Next, we have a little bit of configuration to do. So go ahead and navigate to the src/main/resources and open up the application.properties.

application.properties
server.port=9000
spring.application.name=weather-service
eureka.client.service-url.defaultZone=http://localhost:8761/eureka

In the application.properties, first we're going to set the server.port, and we're going to set that to 9000. And then we're going to set the spring.application.name property, and we're going to set that to weather-service. And the last property we're going to set is the location of the Service Discovery Server. So set that long eureka.client property equal to localhost:8761/eureka. We're now finished with the weather service, so let's quickly start it up and make sure that everything works. So go ahead and close both of those files and open up the discovery-server. Navigate to that main application class, right-click on it, go to Run As, choose Spring Boot App. Once the Service Discovery Server is started, navigate to the main application class of the weather-service, right-click on it, Run As, Spring Boot App. Next, open up a web browser and visit localhost:9000/weather.

sunny

And just make sure that you get a response here. You can refresh it a few times to see that you get various responses. And now that we have our weather service working, let's head back to the IDE and utilize it within our weather app.

```
∨ ᴹ⁵ weather-app [boot]
  > 🔗 Spring Elements
  ∨ 🗁 src/main/java
    ∨ 🔲 io.ajay.kumar.weatherapp
      > 🗎 WeatherAppApplication.java
  > 🗁 src/main/resources
  > 🗁 src/test/java
  > 📚 JRE System Library [JavaSE-1.8]
  > 📚 Maven Dependencies
  > 🗁 src
  > 🗁 target
    📄 mvnw
    📄 mvnw.cmd
    📄 pom.xml
```

Back within your IDE, expand the weather-app and navigate to the main application class. Within the main application class, we're going to define three new annotations.
package io.ajay.kumar.weatherapp;
import
org.springframework.boot.SpringApplication;
import
org.springframework.boot.autoconfigure.Spri ngBootApplication;
import
org.springframework.cloud.client.circuitbreak er.EnableCircuitBreaker;
import
org.springframework.cloud.client.discovery.E nableDiscoveryClient;
import
org.springframework.cloud.client.loadbalance r.LoadBalanced;

181

```java
import
org.springframework.context.annotation.Bean
;
import
org.springframework.web.bind.annotation.Re
stController;
import
org.springframework.web.client.RestTemplat
e;
@SpringBootApplication
@EnableCircuitBreaker
@EnableDiscoveryClient
@RestController
public class WeatherAppApplication {
    public static void main(String[] args) {
        SpringApplication.run(WeatherApp
Application.class, args);
    }
    @Bean
    @LoadBalanced
    public RestTemplate restTemplate() {
        return new RestTemplate();
    }
}
```

The first one is the @EnableCircuitBreaker
annotation, the next one is the
@EnableDiscoveryClient annotation, and the
last one is the @RestController annotation.
Next, we'll define a RestTemplate so that we
can call our weather service, so come down
here and say public RestTempate and call it
restTemplate. Annotate it with the @Bean
annotation and the @LoadBalanced
annotation. And then, in the body of the
method, return a new RestTemplate. Now
remember a Hystrix command can only be
defined in an @Component or an @Service
class, so let's go up here and create a new

class. So right-click, go to New, choose Class, and we'll call this the WeatherService.

```
package io.ajay.kumar.weatherapp;
import javax.inject.Inject;
import org.springframework.stereotype.Service;
import org.springframework.web.client.RestTemplate;
import com.netflix.hystrix.contrib.javanica.annotation.HystrixCommand;
@Service
public class WeatherService {
    @Inject
    private RestTemplate restTemplate;
    @HystrixCommand(fallbackMethod = "unknown")
    public String getWeather() {
        return
restTemplate.getForEntity("http://weather-service/weather",
                    String.class)
                    .getBody();
    }
    public String unknown() {
        return "unknown";
    }
}
```

At the top of the class, go ahead and annotate it with @Service. And then next we'll need our RestTemplate, so private RestTemplate restTemplate. And make sure that we @Inject that. And next, we're going to need a method to call our weather service, so come below this and type public String getWeather. Then, in the body of the method, we'll return restTemplate.getForEntity. And the URL we'll use is http://weather-service/weather.

And then the response type will be a string, so we'll say String.class. And then we'll make sure we call a .getBody to get the response body. This is the method we'll want to annotate with our Hystrix command. So come up to the top of the method and type @HystrixCommand, and we'll use a fallbackMethod called unknown. And then we'll want to make sure that we define that method, so come below the getWeather method and define a new method, public String unknown. And this will be a real simple method. It will just return the string unknown. And just to be crystal clear, we're going to use this WeatherService in our main application class to get the actual weather. And if there's a problem getting the weather, or the WeatherService is down, it'll call that fallbackMethod and just return unknown for the weather. Let's head back to the main application class and use the WeatherService.

```
@SpringBootApplication
@EnableCircuitBreaker
@EnableDiscoveryClient
@RestController
public class WeatherAppApplication {

    @Inject
    private WeatherService weatherService;
    public static void main(String[] args) {
        SpringApplication.run(WeatherApp
Application.class, args);
    }

    @GetMapping("/current/weather")
    public String getWeather() {
        return "The current weather is " +
weatherService.getWeather();
    }
```

184

```
@Bean
@LoadBalanced
public RestTemplate restTemplate() {
    return new RestTemplate();
}
}
```

So back within the main application class, define a new instance variable, private WeatherService, and we'll call that weatherService. And then don't forget to add the @Inject annotation. Then we'll add a new method called getWeather. So come below the main method here and do public String getWeather. And then we're going to return a string here that says the current weather is, and then we'll call the weatherService and get the weather. And this is our handler method, so we'll need the @GetMapping. So define an @GetMapping on the top of this method, and then we'll say the URL is /current/weather. And that's all we need for the code portion of our weather app, so go ahead and close both of these files and navigate to src/main/resources and open up that application.properties.

application.properties
server.port=8000
spring.application.name=weather-app
eureka.client.service-url.defaultZone=http://localhost:8761/eureka

The properties for the weather app are very similar to the ones in the weather service, so I've just copied and pasted those over here. And then we're just going to change some of those values. So for the server.port, we'll change that to 8000, and for the spring.application.name, we'll change that to weather-app. We're ready to start our weather app, so go ahead and close that file and open up the Console. Just go ahead and double-check that your discovery server and your weather service are still running, and then come over to the main WeatherAppApplication class, right-click on it, go to Run As, and choose Spring Boot App. Next, open up a web browser and visit localhost:8000/current/weather.

← → C ⓘ localhost:8000/current/weather

The current weather is rainy

And you should get a response here. And you can refresh it a couple times to see the different values. And next, what we're going to do is we're going to shut down the weather service. And we'll see that Hystrix takes over and recognizes that the weather service is down and returns our fallback method. So we should be able to see the current weather is unknown after we shut down the weather service. So we're back within the IDE, and we have the weather service pulled up in the Console. We'll go ahead and stop the weather service and head back to the browser. Back within the browser, we'll go ahead and refresh the page, and we can see instantly that the current weather is unknown.

← → C ⓘ localhost:8000/current/weather

The current weather is unknown

Hystrix has realized the call to the weather service is failing and it should use its fallback method.

Metrics and Insight with the Hystrix Dashboard

Netflix Hystrix tracks the execution status of protected calls so that it knows when to trip the circuit breaker. And one of the advantages of this is that we can use those metrics to get insight into how our calls are functioning. Reading those metrics in their raw form wouldn't be very easy or efficient. And that's where the Hystrix Dashboard comes in. And the dashboard is a web application that helps you visualize all of those metrics in a quick and easy-to-use fashion. The dashboard is jam-packed with information.

- Tracks metrics such as
  - Circuit state
  - Error rate
  - Traffic volume
  - Successful requests
  - Rejected requests
  - Timeouts
  - Latency percentiles
- Monitor protected calls
  - Single server or cluster

It tracks and displays information about the state of the circuit, whether it's open or closed, the error rate for the call, the traffic volume that it's receiving, how many requests were successful, rejected, or timed out, and the latency percentiles for the call. And you can also use it to track a single server or a cluster of servers. To use it, it's literally as easy as declaring a couple dependencies in your pom.xml and adding a single annotation.

Using Spring Cloud and the Netflix Hystrix Dashboard

In order to use the Hystrix Dashboard, you first, like always, declare a new dependency within the dependencyManagement section of your pom.xml on spring-cloud-dependencies.
pom.xml

```
<dependencyManagement>
  <dependencies>
    <dependency>
      <groupId>org.springframework.cloud
</groupId>
      <artifactId>spring-cloud-
dependencies</artifactId>
      <version>Camden.SR2</version>
      <type>pom</type>
      <scope>import</scope>
    </dependency>
  </dependencies>
</dependencyManagement>
```

And, as always again, make sure that it's of type pom and has a scope of import.
pom.xml

```
<dependency>
<groupId>org.springframework.cloud</groupId>
<artifactId>spring-cloud-starter-hystrix-
dashboard</artifactId>
</dependency>
```

Then, still within your pom.xml, in the dependency section, define a new dependency on spring-cloud-starter-hystrix-dashboard. And finally, you can probably guess it, add the @EnableHystrixDashboard annotation.
@SpringBootApplication

```
@EnableHystrixDashboard
public class Application{
        public static void main(String[]args){
                SpringApplication.run(Applicat
        ion.class,args);
        }
}
```
And that's all you need to get started with the
Hystrix Dashboard.

Reading and Understanding the Hystrix Dashboard

Before we get started with the demo of setting
up the Hystrix Dashboard, it'll be important
to understand how to read the dashboard as it
contains a lot of information in a very small
amount of space.

Circuit

Sort: Error then Volume I Alphabetical I Volume I Error I Mean I Median I 90 I 99 I 99.5

Success I Short-Circuited I Bad Request I Timeout I Rejected I Failure I Error %

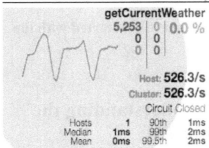

		getCurrentWeather		
		5,253	0	0.0 %
		0	0	
		0	0	

Host: **526.3/s**

Cluster: **526.3/s**

Circuit Closed

Hosts	1	90th	1ms
Median	1ms	99th	2ms
Mean	0ms	99.5th	2ms

Thread Pools   Sort: Alphabetical I Volume I

WeatherService

Host: **525.1/s**

Cluster: **525.1/s**

Active	0	Max Active	1
Queued	0	Executions	5,251
Pool Size	10	Queue Size	5

We'll focus on the top half under the Circuit heading as the bottom half, the Thread Pools, is pretty self-explanatory. The dashboard is quite literally jam-packed with information. And it can be a little daunting when you see it at first, so let's break it down by parts. At the top right you have the name of the Hystrix call that is being protected, and in this picture it's the getCurrentWeather call.

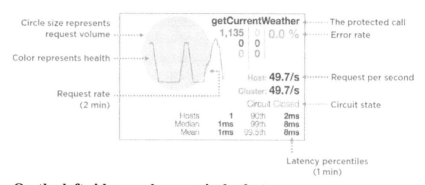

On the left side, you have a circle that represents both the request volume, as well as the health of the call. And the larger the circle gets, the more the request volume is, and the more red the circle becomes, the more unhealthy the call is. Then on top of the circle, the line is a depiction of the request rate over the last 2 minutes. Back on the right side, beneath the name of the protected call in gray, is the error rate of the call. And below that you have the number that indicates the request per second at the host level, as well as at the cluster level. Continuing downward, still on the right side, you have the state of the circuit for this particular call and whether it's open and rejecting traffic or whether it's closed and accepting traffic. And then right below that you have the latency percentiles for this call. Moving back to the top, underneath the name of the protected call are a bunch of numbers in columns with different colors. Let's zoom in on this particular area so we can explain each of these individually. For the numbers, we'll move column by column and row by row. And, just in case you forget, there's a legend at the top of the Hystrix Dashboard that looks just like this.

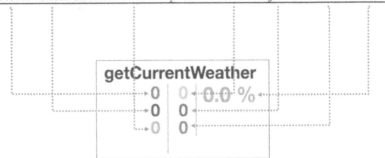

Starting at the first column in the first row, the dark green number represents the number of successful requests. And right below that, the blue number represents the number of short-circuited requests. And these are the requests that didn't even attempt to execute because the circuit was open. Still in the first column, on the bottom row, the light green number represents the number of bad requests. And these requests are errors, but they're not necessarily due to an execution failure. They're due to something like an illegal argument. Moving on to the second column, the first row, the orange number represents the number of timed out requests. And these are requests where the execution was attempted, but a response was not received in the allotted amount of time. Right below the timed out request, the purple number represents the number of rejected requests. And rejected requests happen when there are no more resources to serve a request, either via the thread pool or a semaphore. And remember that the request is rejected so that requests don't stack up at the caller and consume those valuable resources. And the last number in the second column, the red one, is the number of failed requests. And these are requests that failed to execute because they threw an exception. Now that we've got a firm understanding of how to read the Hystrix Dashboard, let's set up and enable our own so that we can visualize some of the metrics that are being admitted from the call that we protected with Hystrix in our previous demo.

Demo: Monitoring Fault Tolerance Metrics with Hystrix Dashboard

In this demo, we'll utilize the Hystrix Dashboard to view some of the metrics of the Hystrix-protected call from the weather app to the weather service. First things first, if your services and your discovery server aren't already running, you'll need to start each of them up. And we'll start with the discovery server first. So expand the discovery-server project and navigate to the main application class. Right-click on it, go to Run As, and choose Spring Boot App. Repeat that same process for the weather service and then the weather app. The weather service and the weather app and the discovery server are all running. And just to double-check, you can click little caret and see that each of those services is started. Next, go ahead and open up a web browser so we can create and download the Hystrix Dashboard project. In your web browser, visit start.spring.io. In the Group section, use io.ajay.kumar, and then for the artifact name we'll say hystrix-dashboard. And then for the dependencies, we'll type Hystrix Dashboard.

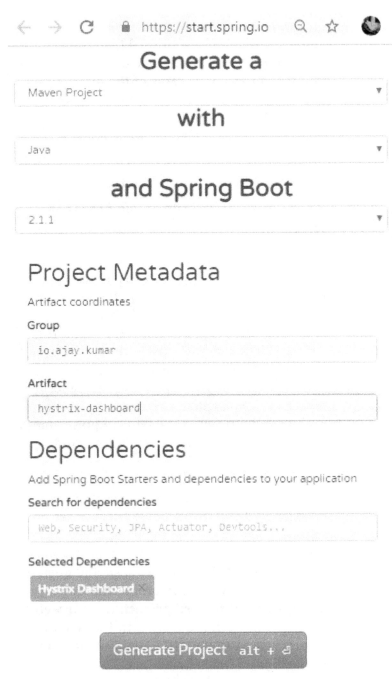

Once you have everything filled out, go ahead and click the Generate Project button, and that'll create and download that zip file for

you. Like always, extract that zip file and head back to your IDE. Back within your IDE, right-click on the empty space in the Package Explorer, go to Import, choose Existing Maven Projects, click Next, click Browse, locate the downloaded zip file, and click Open, and click Finish.

- hystrix-dashboard [boot]
  - Spring Elements
  - src/main/java
    - io.ajay.kumar.hystrixdashboard
      - HystrixDashboardApplication.java
  - src/main/resources
  - src/test/java
  - JRE System Library [JavaSE-1.8]
  - Maven Dependencies
  - src
  - target
  - mvnw
  - mvnw.cmd
  - pom.xml

Expand the Hystrix Dashboard project and navigate to the main application class.
package io.ajay.kumar.hystrixdashboard;
import
org.springframework.boot.SpringApplication;
import
org.springframework.boot.autoconfigure.Spri
ngBootApplication;
import
org.springframework.cloud.netflix.hystrix.das
hboard.EnableHystrixDashboard;
@SpringBootApplication
@EnableHystrixDashboard
public class HystrixDashboardApplication {
    public static void main(String[] args) {
SpringApplication.run(HystrixDashboardApp
lication.class, args);
    }

195

}

Within the main application class, we will quite literally add one annotation, and that's the @EnableHystrixDashboard annotation. Next, we're ready to start things up and view the dashboard. So on the main application class, right-click on it, go to Run As, choose Spring Boot App. Next, open up a browser and visit localhost:8080/hystrix.

Hystrix Dashboard

http://hostname:port/turbine/turbine.stream

Cluster via Turbine (default cluster): http://turbine-hostname:port/turbine.stream
Cluster via Turbine (custom cluster): http://turbine-hostname:port/turbine.stream?cluster=[clusterName]
Single Hystrix App: http://hystrix-app:port/actuator/hystrix.stream

Delay: 2000   ms   Title: Example Hystrix App

Monitor Stream

This should load up the Hystrix Dashboard. And before we view any metrics, we'll need to actually generate some metrics. So open up a new tab and visit your weather app at localhost:8000/current/weather.

   ⓘ localhost:8000/current/weather

The current weather is sunny

And just go ahead and refresh that a few times to get some metrics generated. Back at the Hystrix Dashboard, we'll put in the URL to the Hystrix stream of our weather app. So that's http://localhost:8000/hystrix.stream. And for the title of our dashboard, we'll say

Weather App. Next, click the Monitor Stream button, and you should be presented with some metrics.

If you don't see metrics right away, you can flip back and forth between your weather app and refreshing it to generate some metrics and back to the dashboard to see the effect of those requests.

Aggregating Hystrix Metrics with Netflix Turbine

Hystrix metrics are tracked on a service-by-service basis. Now a single Hystrix stream might have metrics on more than one Hystrix protected call, but those metrics are only for that service. And the implications of this are that every service has its own Hystrix stream URL that you need to use if you want to consume its metrics. If you wanted to track the metrics for multiple services, you'd have to open up multiple Hystrix Dashboards and track them independently. And I'm sure you can imagine how big of a pain that would be if you had tens or even hundreds of services that made up your application. To solve this, Netflix developed a tool called Turbine that aggregates many Hystrix streams into one. To give you a better understanding of how this might look, let's look at a screenshot from the Hystrix Dashboard.

getCurrentWeather				getCurrentDatetime		
0	0	0.0 %		0	0	0.0 %
0	0			0	0	
0	0			0	0	

Host: **0.0/s**   Host: **0.0/s**
Cluster: **0.0/s**   Cluster: **0.0/s**
Circuit Closed   Circuit Closed

Hosts	1	90th	0ms	Hosts	1	90th	0ms
Median	0ms	99th	0ms	Median	0ms	99th	0ms
Mean	0ms	99.5th	0ms	Mean	0ms	99.5th	0ms

Stream located at `localhost:8080`

Stream located at `localhost:8181`

In the screenshot, you can see there are two protected calls, the getCurrentWeather call and the getCurrentDatetime call. And the protected call on the left is from a service located on localhost:8080, and the one on the right is from another service located on localhost:8181. And Turbine has brought both of these metrics together from different services, all viewable in the same dashboard.

Using Spring Cloud and Netflix Turbine

So how do we start using Turbine? Well, if you've been following along throughout the book, you can probably already guess.
pom.xml
<dependencyManagement>
  <dependencies>
    <dependency>
      <groupId>org.springframework.cloud</groupId>
      <artifactId>spring-cloud-dependencies</artifactId>

198

```xml
<version>Camden.SR2</version>
<type>pom</type><scope>import</sco
pe>
    </dependency>
  </dependencies>
</dependencyManagement>
```

You start by defining a new dependency on spring-cloud-dependencies in the dependencyManagement section of your pom.xml. As always, make sure that it's of type pom and has a scope of import.

pom.xml

```xml
<dependency>
<groupId>org.springframework.cloud</groupId>
<artifactId>spring-cloud-starter-turbine</artifactId>
</dependency>
```

Then, still within your pom.xml, in the dependency section, define a new dependency on spring-cloud-starter-turbine. Follow that up by adding a new annotation to your main Application class, the @EnableTurbine annotation.

```java
@SpringBootApplication
@EnableTurbine
public class Application{
        public static void main(String[]args){
                SpringApplication.run(Application.class,args);
        }
}
```

And last, we have a little bit of configuration to add. In your application.properties or your application.yml, we're going to add two new properties.

application.properties

```
turbine.app-config=<list_of_service_ids>
turbine.cluster-name-expression='default'
```

199

OR
application.ymlturbine:appConfig:<list_of_se
rvice_ids>
clusterNameExpression:"'default'"
* In addition to the standard spring
application name and discovery server
location properties
The first property is the turbine.app-config
property, and you set this to a comma-
separated list of service IDs. And these are the
same service IDs that you use for service
discovery. The second property, the
turbine.cluster-name-expression property, can
be a Spring Expression Language value to
name your cluster. And in Turbine, a cluster
is just a grouping of services that need to be
monitored together. And for our purposes, to
make things easy, we're going to set that value
to default surrounded by single quotes. And a
note here is if you're using YAML instead of
properties, you'll need to escape the single
quotes with double quotes.

Hystrix Dashboard

http://hostname:port/turbine.stream

Once you have everything configured and your Hystrix Dashboard is started up, instead of entering the hystrix.stream URL, you'd enter the URL of your Turbine server and end it with turbine.stream. Let's apply the stuff we learned by created our own Turbine server, and we can use it to aggregate the stream of our service we created in the previous demo along with a new service.

Demo: Aggregating Multiple Hystrix Streams with Turbine

In this demo, we'll utilize Turbine to combine the Hystrix streams from two different services so that they're both viewable from the

201

same Hystrix Dashboard. We'll continue to utilize the weather app, the weather service, and the discovery server from our previous demo, and then we'll add two new projects that you can clone from GitHub. The first new project is the datetime-service, and you can get that from github.com/ajaycucek/hystrix-datetime-service. And the second new project is the datetime-app. And you can get that, again, at github.com/ajaycucek/hystrix-datetime-app. Once you've cloned both of those projects, make sure that you import them into your IDE. I've imported mine, and your IDE should look pretty similar to this. The two new projects, the datetime-app and the datetime-service, are literally identical to the weather app and the weather service, with the exception that they return the current datetime instead of the weather. So feel free to browse around and check out the code for those. We'll need to start each of these applications starting with the discovery server first. Again, I have all of the applications started. And once they're all started up, you can verify by clicking little caret and making sure that all of the applications show up. With all of the applications started, we'll go ahead and start building our Netflix Turbine app. Open up a browser and visit start.spring.io. In the Group use io.ajay.kumar, and for the artifact name you can just call it turbine. And for the dependencies, we'll obviously want to add Turbine.

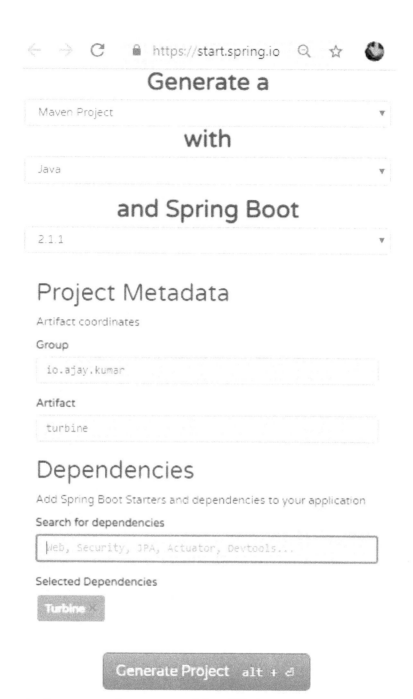

And once you have everything filled out, click that Generate Project button, and that'll create and download that zip file for you. And,

like always, unzip that zip file and import that into your IDE. We're back within the IDE where we've imported the Turbine project.

- turbine [boot]
  - Spring Elements
  - src/main/java
    - io.ajay.kumar.turbine
      - TurbineApplication.java
  - src/main/resources
  - src/test/java
  - JRE System Library [JavaSE-1.8]
  - Maven Dependencies
  - src
  - target
  - mvnw
  - mvnw.cmd
  - pom.xml

Go ahead and expand the project and navigate to the main application class.

```
package io.ajay.kumar.turbine;
import
org.springframework.boot.SpringApplication;
import
org.springframework.boot.autoconfigure.Spri
ngBootApplication;
import
org.springframework.cloud.netflix.turbine.En
ableTurbine;
@SpringBootApplication
@EnableTurbine
public class TurbineApplication {
    public static void main(String[] args) {
        SpringApplication.run(TurbineAppl
ication.class, args);
    }
}
```

In the main application class, we'll add one new annotation, and that's the @EnableTurbine annotation. Next, we'll need

to configure some properties, so go ahead and close that file and navigate to src/main/resources, application.properties.
application.properties
server.port=3000
spring.application.name=turbine-aggregator
eureka.client.service-url.defaultZone=http://localhost:8761/eureka
turbine.app-config=weather-app,datetime-app
turbine.cluster-name-expression='default'
In the application.properties, we have a number of different properties to set, so I'm going to go ahead and paste those in here, and then we're going to go through each one of them one by one. The first property, the server.port, we're going to set that to 3000. The next property, the application.name, we're going to call turbine-aggregator. And then the third property, the eureka.client.service-url, set that to localhost:8761/eureka. And then below that, we have the two turbine properties. And remember the first one, the turbine.app-config property, sets the applications or services that you want Turbine to aggregate together as a stream. In our case, we want the weather-app and the datetime-app. And then the last property, the turbine.cluster-name-expression, we just set that to default surrounded by single quotes. And that's all for our properties, so go ahead and close that file, and then we're going to go ahead and start the Turbine application. So come over to the main application class, right-click on it, go to Run As, and choose Spring Boot App. Next, open up a web browser, and we're going to visit the datetime app and the weather app to generate some metrics for their Hystrix streams so that Turbine can them collect them. So let's visit

the datetime app first. So go to localhost:4000/current/datetime.

← → C ⟳ localhost:4000/current/datetime

___

The date/time is Mon Feb 20 21:11:14 MDT 2018

And just refresh that a few times to generate some metrics. And then we're going to do the same thing for the weather service, so go to localhost:8000/current/weather, and then also refresh that a few times to generate some metrics.

← → C ⓘ localhost:8000/current/weather

___

The current weather is rainy

Next, open up a New Tab and visit localhost:8080/hystrix.

Hystrix Dashboard

http://localhost:3000/turbine.stream

Cluster via Turbine (default cluster): http://turbine-hostname:port/turbine.stream
Cluster via Turbine (custom cluster): http://turbine-hostname:port/turbine.stream?cluster=[clusterName]
Single Hystrix App: http://hystrix-app:port/hystrix.stream

Delay: 2000   ms   Title: Turbine

Monitor Stream

And this time, instead of putting in the hystrix.stream URL, we'll use the turbine.stream URL. So go ahead and type http://localhost:3000/turbine.stream. And then in the Title textbox just type Turbine. After that, click the Monitor Stream button, and you should see metrics from the datetime app,

that's the getCurrentDateTime call, and you should also see metrics from the weather app, and that's the getWeather call.

And if you don't, just go back to those services and refresh them a few times to generate some metrics.

Summary

We're at the end of this module so, like always, let's do a recap of what we learned.
- Fault tolerance is a requirement
- Netflix Hystrix
  - Circuit breaker pattern
  - @HystrixCommand &
  - @EnableCircuitBreaker
- Netflix Hystrix Dashboard & Turbine
  - Monitor one or several streams

First, we saw that failures in a distributed system are pretty much inevitable. And we have to learn to embrace failures and make handling failures a requirement. Then we introduced Netflix Hystrix, which is an implementation of the Circuit Breaker pattern, among other fault-tolerance patterns. And we saw how to use the @EnableCircuitBreaker annotation and the @HystrixCommand annotation to protect a call that might fail. We concluded the module by looking at how we can visualize and monitor our Hystrix-protected calls with the Hystrix Dashboard and how we can monitor several streams at once with Turbine.

Module 8: Bringing It All Together and Where to Go Next

Introduction

In this last module we'll take a holistic approach to see how each of the individual ideas and technologies all fit together and where you can go next after you've completed the book.

- How does it all fit together?
  - Service Discovery
  - Distributed Configuration
  - Client-side load balancing
  - Gateway and routing
  - Fault tolerance and circuit breaker
- What's next?
  - Other Spring Cloud Projects

We'll begin with a section on how it all fits together. We've learned a lot throughout the book covering new ideas and technologies in every single module. And while many of those ideas are useful by themselves, the real advantage comes from using them together as a whole. And we'll see how each of the main topics, service discovery, distributed configuration, client-side load balancing, gateway and routing, and fault tolerance and circuit breaker, all fit together to form a cloud-native system. And then, like I mentioned, we'll finish by briefly discussing where you can go next to learn about what additional Spring Cloud projects are out there. And don't discount the importance of this. It's helpful to know exactly what's out there. It's almost like browsing the tool section at your local hardware store, and if you don't know what tools are out there, when you have a problem, you might end up using the wrong tool for the wrong job.

How Does It All Fit Together?

The question is how does it all fit together to form a cloud-native system? And, to start, let's recap everything that's involved. It all starts with one or more application services.

```
        ┌─────────────┐
        │  Discovery  │
        └─────────────┘

┌──────────┐              ┌──────────┐
│ Gateway  │              │  Config  │
└──────────┘              └──────────┘

     ┌───────────┐ ┌───────────┐
     │ Service A │ │ Service B │
     └───────────┘ └───────────┘
```

And in our example here we have two application services, application Service A and application Service B, and both of them are running multiple instances. Then, at the heart of everything is the Service Discovery Server.

It's the phonebook or the directory of the system allowing everyone to register their location, as well as discover the location of others. And remember that we utilized Netflix Eureka throughout the book for our service discovery needs. Next, we have the Config Server to handle our dynamic and distributed configuration needs. And remember that we use the Spring Cloud Config Server for this. After that, we have the gateway, or the front door, of the system, and it's responsible for receiving and routing requests to back-end services. And we use Netflix Zuul for this. Then we have a client-side load balancer to distribute requests among the multiple instances that we run for high availability purposes. And remember in our case we used Netflix Ribbon. And last, we have fault tolerance to be able to tolerate and measure failures and prevent them from causing cascading failures to other systems. And we use Netflix Hystrix for this.

Putting It All Together: On Startup

Now that we've recapped all of the pieces involved, let's take a moment to look at how they all interact with each other, specifically on startup.

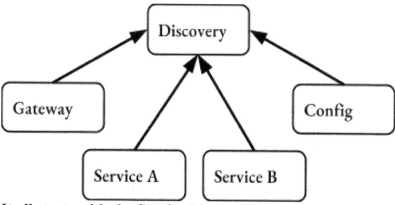

It all starts with the Service Discovery Server.
Each and every instance of every piece of the
system registers itself with the Service
Discovery Server upon startup. And then it
also receives a reply with the location of other
registered services. For application services,
this reply is very important because it tells
them where the location of the Configuration
Server is at.

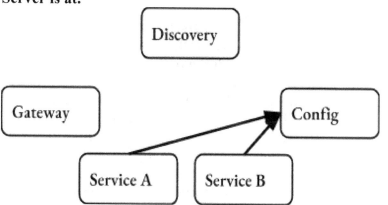

And once they know the location of the
Configuration Server, they can make a
request to retrieve any configuration that will
ultimately be used to bootstrap their startup
process.

Putting It All Together: On Request

Now that we have all of our application and their supporting services started, let's look at how they all interact with each other during a request.

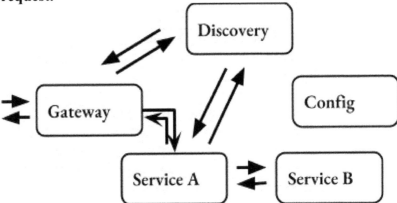

The request for a given path begins at the gateway server, Netflix Zuul in our case. And Zuul will match the path to a given service ID, and then it will use service discovery, either by requesting it from the Service Discovery Server or via a previously cached result, to locate the service that will handle that path. Once the service is located, it'll make a Hystrix-protected call to the service using Ribbon to handle the client-side load balancing of which instances it should send the traffic to. In our example, the request was sent to Service A. Now, suppose that Service A also depends on Service B to fulfill the request. Upon receiving the request, Service A will utilize service discovery to locate Service B. And it'll do that either via a previously cached result or by requesting it from the Service

Discovery Server. Next, it'll make a Hystrix-protected call using Ribbon for client-side load balancing to one of the instances of Service B. Service B will respond to Service A, and then Service A will respond to the gateway, and finally, the gateway will respond to the original request.

Where to Go Next

Throughout the book, we've covered the core fundamentals of Spring Cloud and given you a good foundation to build upon.
Fundamentals we covered, they only represent two of the many pieces of Spring Cloud.

- Spring Cloud Config
- Spring Cloud Netflix

And remember that Spring Cloud is a conglomerate of projects, and while the fundamentals that we covered was a lot of information to learn, they only represent two of the many pieces of Spring Cloud. And that's the Spring Cloud Config project and the Spring Cloud Netflix project.

- Spring Cloud
  - Spring Cloud Bus
  - Spring Cloud Task
  - Spring Cloud Cluster
  - Spring Cloud Consul
  - Spring Cloud Sleuth
  - Spring Cloud Security
  - Spring Cloud Stream
  - More...

There are a whole bunch of other projects like Spring Cloud Bus, Spring Cloud Cluster, and Spring Cloud Stream that all help you solve problems in the cloud. To get the best idea of what's available with Spring Cloud, visit the documentation page at http://projects.spring.io/spring-cloud, and then scroll down to the section with the heading Main Projects. Here you'll find all of the Spring Cloud projects that sit under the Spring Cloud umbrella. And I encourage you to check them out, if only so that you're familiar with them and you know that they exist because, like I mentioned before, it can be really helpful to know what tools exist so that you use the right tool for the right job.